THE ULTIMATE GUIDE TO SOLO AND SMALL FIRM SUCCESS

D1417679

THE ULTIMATE GUIDE TO SOLO AND SMALL FIRM SUCCESS

Renée Caggiano Berman

LawFirst Publishing
The Connecticut Bar Association
New Britain, CT

2009

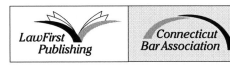

LawFirst Publishing
The Connecticut Bar Association

First published in 2009 by LawFirst Publishing
A division of the Connecticut Bar Association

ISBN 0-9740069-8-X

Printed in the United States of America
15 14 13 12 11 10 09   1 2 3 4 5 6

Edited by: Lewis K. Parker, Editor
             Emma L. Gormley, Associate Editor

The Connecticut Bar Association
30 Bank Street
PO Box 350
New Britain, CT 06050-0350

Contents

FOREWORD

Over the last two decades, BigLaw has led many to believe the legal profession operates outside the economic rules governing the rest of the world. Just a few years ago, we read about first-year associates receiving astronomical annual salaries upwards of $200,000, sixth-year associates making $300,000, and partners earning $1 million or more. But today we know that the legal profession is no different than any other profession. In the midst of the stock market implosion and shakeout and the infamous "Bloody Thursday" on February 12, 2009, the profession is cluttered with out-of-work associates and partners wandering the streets dazed and confused. This is due in part to both the system's own structural flaws and our unprecedented national and global economic crisis.

And the other sad reality: Law schools don't teach their students the business end—or shall I say, the entrepreneurial end, of being a lawyer. Why? It's no secret, really. Teaching students how to start a solo practice, especially right out of law school, doesn't serve their agenda. That is a disservice to the paying customer. Their goal is simple: job placement and employment within the first nine months. Let someone else teach graduates the practice of law and how to run a business. They get you in, take your money, try to get you into a job, any job, within nine months. By doing so, the *U.S. News and World Reports* will smile favorably upon the school, hopefully increasing the all-important ranking. There are more than 43,000 law school students graduating each year. What percentage are actually getting decent paying jobs (especially in this economy) if they choose to be employed? And are the jobs realistically within reach? Does (or did) your law school's agenda help you to achieve your goals?

If statistics are tortured long enough, they will tell the statistician whatever they want to hear, but it is generally known that more than half of all lawyers leave the profession. In addition, the number of lawyers who fall into depression or become addicted to drugs or alcohol is staggering. How much is due to dissatisfaction, not in practicing law but in the way they are practicing law? Again, statistics vary, but the undeniable truth is the largest percentage of private practitioners in the United States are solo practitioners, yet they remain the unsung heroes of our profession seldom recognized for their commitment to the profession and their incredible innovation. But the most important question: What do YOU really want when you map out your life for the next two or three or four decades? This book is about helping those with a legal degree who desire to practice law become an entrepreneur. Whether you are currently in school planning to open your own business upon passing the bar exam, a young new lawyer ready to take the plunge, a talented and passionate mature lawyer who doesn't anticipate being employable nor wants to be an employee, or a veteran ready to try your hand at hanging a shingle, this book is for you because the concerns are universal: How do I do it? Where will I get clients? Law school never taught me the business end of being a lawyer.

If you are reading this book, chances are you fall into one of four categories. You are:

- a student (traditional or non-traditional) who already knows you want to seriously consider the solo option either right out of law school or shortly the reafter
- a new lawyer (out of school less than three years) who either can't get the job you want or just wanted to get your feet wet first before striking out on your own;
- a veteran lawyer (practicing more than three years) who now wants to strike out on your own after years of working for another and/or feels you have no future or stability in your current employment and you've defined going solo as the only option
- a current solo practitioner who wants tips on how to improve your practice

Some people say it doesn't matter why you are starting a solo practice. I disagree. It does matter why you are going into solo practice because your attitude about your choice (and everything in life is a choice) will color your entire professional career. It will determine your financial and personal success as an entrepreneur in the legal profession. What doesn't matter is how you got to the final decision. But once you've made the decision to go solo, your attitude is everything. Regardless of the economy and in spite of what law school didn't teach you, going solo can be an amazing journey. Small, agile, able to make decisions quickly and holding little baggage, solos have traditionally been far ahead of the curve. Hard work? Yes. But great enterprises have always been built upon the ashes of great collapses. Isn't it time you created your enterprise?

Attorney Susan Cartier Liebel is the founder of Solo Practice University, the "practice of law" school— a Web-based educational and professional networking community for lawyers and law students. She is an attorney who started her own practice right out of law school, an adjunct professor at Quinnipiac University School of Law for eight years, teaching law students how to open their own legal practices right out of law school, and a columnist for the Connecticut Law Tribune, Lawyers USA Weekly, *and* The Complete Lawyer, *writing on issues facing solos. She can be reached at susan@solopracticeuniversity.com.*

PREFACE

"Look at a day when you are supremely satisfied at the end. It's not a day when you lounge around doing nothing; it's when you had everything to do, and you've done it."
—*Margaret Thatcher*

A story and a dream are usually what we all have in common. "We" meaning all of us who have dared to open our own practice. Some of us had no choice because there were no job offers. Some of us dreamed of building a large firm, one attorney at a time. Some of us just wanted more flexibility and thought being our own boss would grant us such luxuries. Those who decide to hang out their shingles often are entrepreneurs down to their core. If you ask any solo practitioner at what age they first tested the waters of self-employment, many will recall childhood memories of such endeavors. As a child, I optimized my lemonade stand success by testing location, poster board placement, and gimmicks such as free cookies with each glass. As a teenager, I started a babysitting service and handed fliers out to mothers as they whisked their children to my neighbor's pool for swim class. Being my own boss was in my blood and I could not escape its draw.

Most entrepreneurs share a commonality in that they chafe at following rules and restrictions. They would rather make the rules and control their own destiny. As an entrepreneur, the rewards are yours, as are the challenges, but the important point is that they are all yours.

My story goes like this: After law school, I worked for an insurance defense firm for one year. I was fired from this firm three days before I was to assume a hefty mortgage. I then worked for a small family-run practice for three years. I probably would have stayed there indefinitely if life outside of law didn't happen. I was blessed with the birth of my son and instantly my tolerable commute turned me into an enraged rush hour driver as I attempted each evening to get to my son's daycare hoping that he was not the last child as was so often the case. I explored the possibility of finding employment closer to home, but I knew that the only ladder I wanted to be climbing was the one that I used to construct my own endeavors.

I have always been a risk taker. When I was 20 years old, I flung my jumpsuit-clad body out of an airplane at 10,500 feet. So when I was 30 years old, I took another plunge and decided to open my own law practice. This time I didn't need an airplane, but the ride has been just as exhilarating.

The moments of panic now are not much different from the moment the plane hatch opened ten years ago. When I desperately gripped the side of the plane while peering into the vast blue, I questioned my judgment to engage in such a hapless activity. Likewise, my decision to go solo vacillated between clinging onto the familiar and yearning to explore the unknown. Again, I slowly released my white-knuckled grip and cast myself into the unknown, this time better equipped for the invigorating and jarring ride that I was sure would follow. What I did not expect were the equally prevalent moments of serenity and satisfaction that likewise transpired as I began this expedition.

I felt that I was equipped with the tools to be a solo practitioner; that is, from the standpoint of being a lawyer. However, what I did not have were the skills to be a business owner, public relations advisor, marketing director, accountant, office manager, and rainmaker. I learned these ropes by climbing them, one knot at a time.

During my first year open, gratification occurred unexpectedly and during simple moments: overhearing the receptionist answer my phone; driving by my office on the day the new sign is erected; noticing that my file cabinets are no longer filled with office supplies but rather with files; and perhaps, most importantly, realizing that I could go to the Halloween parade at my son's school. Small moments like those eased my doubt, hesitation, and apprehension.

When announcing my decision to go solo, I was met with varying responses. Most people were supportive; however, I did hear a few comments infected with doubt and reservation similar to the comment I heard ten years ago: "What if the parachute doesn't open?" Risk is an unavoidable component to going solo. As a prior adrenaline fanatic, I suppose it was the closest thing I could do to nurture that part of my character since skydiving and bungee jumping were blacklisted from my repertoire of leisurely activities following my son's birth. I remind myself every day that I am not the first person to take this plunge. Many have done it before me. Many will do it after me. Some will succeed brilliantly. Some will falter disappointingly. But all will have experienced the same initial trepidation and elation and I am sure all would have regretted it immensely had they not taken the risk.

Business has been frenzied at times and sluggish on occasion, but relatively constant. There have been moments when my heart palpitated from the anxiety of trying to do it all. I reluctantly admit that I have had to call opposing counsel on the morning of court to plead with him to mark his motion off because my son's daycare was closed due to snow. There have been Friday nights hunched over my desk until 11:00 p.m., so I could catch up on all that was not accomplished the previous week. There have been Sunday mornings spent standing at the copy machine preparing a client's voluminous discovery compliance. There have been moments of eerie silence when it seemed like my office phones would never ring again and moments of complete cacophony when all were ringing at the same time.

At the beginning, I gratefully took on almost every new client who sat across from my new cherry desk because I feared they could be my last for some time. Now I consider each client and his or her case before I slide the retainer agreement across my desk. I know that when a client says she does not have the funds to pay a retainer fee but can make periodic payments, it usually means that they there are not funds to make periodic payments either. Nevertheless, I continue to occasionally take on these cases because I am either a slow learner or an eternal optimist.

As a solo practitioner, life can no longer be compartmentalized into "work" life and "personal" life, but rather these two spheres melt into one another. My son has occupied himself on a Saturday afternoon by plucking the leaves from the plant in my office while I accomplished end-of-the-month billing. Conversely, I have stood in the cereal aisle of the supermarket typing on my BlackBerry® in response to a potential new client's consultation inquiry.

This adventure has been an exhilarating launch with perhaps some clumsy landings along the way; however, I remind myself every day to relish the small accomplishments and enjoy the flight.

For those of you who are likewise gripping the sides of the airplane, ready to take the plunge, I hope this book can be a practical "how to" guide to help you do everything from selecting a name to reconciling your financial statements to probably one of the most elusive concepts for a solo practitioner to grasp: balancing it all, if there is ever such a thing.

This book does not teach passion nor does it define what a successful practice looks like. Those lie within you. Rather, this book focuses on what you need to do and what decisions need to be made before you take on the job of business owner. Although opening your own practice is a risk, it should be a thoroughly planned and calculated risk. To quote the enigmatic, but undoubtedly successful, Stephen King, "Talent is cheaper than table salt. What separates the talented individual from the successful one is a lot of hard work."

ACKNOWLEDGMENTS

There are a multitude of people who made this book possible. If it was not for my editor, Lewis Parker, I never would have had the opportunity to write this book. Thank you for putting your faith in me. Thank you to all of the talented people at LawFirst Publishing who work tirelessly to bring their writers' words to life.

Thank you to my son, Ethan, for inspiring me to take the plunge and think big. Your hugs and kisses are the best part of my day. I love you bigger than the whole sky.

Thank you to the talented individuals who made up my business advisory panel: David Berman of Simone Consultants LLC for his financial proficiency, and more importantly, his continuous friendship; Michael Manzo of Zuted Design for explaining the fast world of the Web at my speed; Kathy McAfee of Kmc Brand Innovation LLC for sharing her contagious passion and energy; Donna Palomba and Steve Harris of The Worx Group for helping me think outside of the box; and L. Kay Wilson for contributing her words of wisdom and strength so that every female attorney can be inspired to greatness. The expertise of these great people helped make this the book I envisioned it to be.

A special thank you goes out to Susan Cartier Liebel for not only writing the Foreword but also for inspiring young lawyers to reach for the stars. Thank you to the ladies at the office who made sure it looked like I was still in business during the all-consuming final days of writing and to Kerriann Pepitone for lightening my workload so I could devote more time to this project.

I owe a collectively big thank you to my family and friends who encouraged me in so many different ways. The pep talks, comic relief, and empathy they offered carried me through the months of writing. I am grateful to be surrounded by so many wonderful people. A special thank you goes out to my parents who always champion my crazy ideas—skydiving, opening my own business, and all the other things that have given them greys through the years. Thank you for your unconditional support.

Last, but certainly not least, Jason, thank you for your patience and support and for always challenging me to push a little further and a little harder.

TAKING THE PLUNGE

"The difference between a successful person and others is not a lack of strength, not a lack of knowledge, but rather a lack of will."
—*Vince Lombardi*

SUCCESS DEFINED

How does one define success? For each, the definition of success is as unique as the person. For some, success is monetary. For others, success is finding personal and professional life balance. Some link success to professional achievement and recognition.

Simply put, success means setting goals and reaching them. Not every goal is long-term or large. You can have daily goals, yearly goals, or lifetime goals. Some goals are more challenging than others. Some goals require personality and behavioral modifications. Most require patience, perseverance, and the willingness to step outside of your comfort zone and take risks. The ultimate goal of a career is psychological success. Psychological success is feeling pride and personal accomplishment that comes from achieving both work-related and personal goals in life.

As a solo practitioner, what is your goal? Will you identify yourself as successful when you settle that six-figure personal injury case or when you attend your child's school play at ten o'clock on a Monday morning? Once you decide to open your own business, you have far greater control over fulfilling your own personal definition of success.

This is your practice, and as the owner, designer, and creator, you can make it into anything you desire. Before you begin the external planning of your solo practice, you must paint an internal vision of what you would like the completed picture to depict. Visualize yourself during a workday at your office. What does it look like? What does it sound like? What does it feel like? Once you answer these questions, then you will gain a better understanding of what a "successful practice" means to you.

Regardless of how you define success, the successful person is also the self-aware person. In other words, what do you think of yourself and who do you think you are?

- ✔ Do you handle challenges and obstacles that you encounter at work?
- ✔ Are you the type of person who would rather hide under your desk than confront a problem?
- ✔ Are you willing to work long hours?
- ✔ Can you accept that you may not take home a paycheck for a long term?
- ✔ Can you handle the stress of being responsible for all business decisions?
- ✔ Can you work independently?
- ✔ Are you disciplined enough to set a schedule for yourself and stick with it?
- ✔ Are you willing to accept multi-roles within your business?

Answering "no" to any of those questions does not mean you will fail as a solo practitioner, but rather it means you may need to adjust your expectations. It also means you will need to accept and address your weaknesses, so they do not overshadow your strengths.

Success can be learned. Discipline and planning are the keys to your success so that you can align your goals with the demands of your practice. Without it, your operation will crumble.

What cannot be learned is passion. Passion is the force that allows you to make your plan a reality. The passion needs to run deeper than dollar signs. Passion runs through your veins and materializes as energy and drive. A person without passion will undoubtedly lack the commitment and motivation to make a solo practice a success and will never truly find fulfillment as a solo practitioner.

GRADUATION TO SOLO PRACTITIONER: CAN YOU?

Can you, yes. Should you, probably not…but do not close this book just yet.

I know attorneys who have done it and who are now succeeding brilliantly, but discussions with those people revealed that they faced challenges above and beyond someone who has a few years' experience under their belt. A newly minted attorney who opts for self-employment needs to figure out how to practice law and how to run a business.

According to a statistical report conducted by the American Bar Foundation, solo practitioners make up 48 percent of the private-practice lawyers. According to a separate 2004 study conducted by the American Bar Foundation, only 5 percent of graduating law students immediately hang shingles upon graduation. I included these statistics not to emphasize the low percentage of graduating students who venture out on their own immediately after graduation, but rather to show that there are attorneys out there who have not allowed fear to dictate their dreams. So is it harder to go straight from law school to solo practitioner? Yes, but it is not impossible.

Most of us learned very little about being a lawyer when we went to law school. As a newly admitted attorney with the memory of blue book final exams still fresh, you probably have better research skills than most seasoned attorneys. Therefore, when a legal question is posed for which you do not know the answer, you will be able to quickly research the law. However, being a lawyer is more than just providing legal answers to legal questions. Yes, there were moot court competitions, legal internships, and writing and research classes, but law school does not teach you local court procedure, how to handle difficult clients, what types of motions to file when, and so on. While some law schools are now offering courses on law practice management, most schools still adhere to the traditional law school curriculum, leaving graduates unprepared to hang a shingle immediately after graduation.

Even more prevalent within a new attorney is doubt, apprehension, and lack of confidence. These emotions often creep into new attorneys' repertoire of emotions when they go to court during the first year out of school, when they negotiate settlements, when they draft a pleading, or when they have a disagreement with a client. We all need to learn these skills at some point, but they are better learned under the tutelage of someone who has a few years behind them.

With that said, you can do it; just equip yourself with the right tools. I suggest you keep your contact list close to you and active. You should have already joined the local bar associations as a student and should have volunteered for every community event, attended every luncheon, and signed up for as many sections and committees as you could. This is how you will build a contact list of other attorneys who will help when you need guidance, advice, or tips on how to navigate the courthouse. Believe it or not, most attorneys will be amenable to helping out an enthusiastic and gracious new attorney. Many attorneys have strong egos and with a little stroking, they will be eager to share their opinions and advice with you. Also, compile a list of law school buddies whom you can call with questions. They will likely not know the answers either, but you can beg them to run the questions by other associates in their firms.

Finding a mentor may be the key to easing your apprehension as you transition from law student to solo practitioner. The *American Heritage Dictionary* defines a mentor as "a wise and trusted counselor or teacher." A mentor should not be the friend who graduated from law school a year before you. A mentor should be someone who has practiced for a few years, someone who has a few trials under their belt, and a few war stories to share. A mentor does not need to have all the answers, but a mentor should know where to direct so you can find the answers to your questions. How do you find a mentor? Perhaps you took a class in law school that was taught by a practicing attorney. Perhaps you connected with another attorney at a local bar association event. Once you have identified someone whom you would like to mentor you, call the person and suggest a lunch meeting. If this individual agrees to mentor you, you should meet in-person once a month to keep the relationship fresh. Be appreciative of the wisdom and insight that a mentor offers by dropping quick notes on occasion, expressing thanks for the time the mentor shared with you.

Be aware that as a new attorney, it will take you twice and sometimes three times as long to draft pleadings, discovery, and even correspondence. Do not penalize your clients because they retained an attorney with little experience. You should not be billing your clients for all of this time, and I assure you they will not be happy to hear that you billed them two hours for a pleading that consisted of ten sentences, a copy of which you should have sent to your clients.

While some potential clients might balk at retaining an inexperienced attorney, others might be energized by having a fresh, passionate, and energetic advocate on their side. You are going to need to make your passion speak louder than your inexperience.

LAW PRACTICE OR BUSINESS?

The legal profession is a living organism that changes, grows, and evolves. As attorneys, we never reach perfection, but rather we strive to perfect our skills throughout our career; hence why it is coined "the practice of law." However, when we make the decision to open our own office, we are also making the decision to become a business owner. Our profession is such that it allows us to hang our shingle as soon as we receive our diploma, but unfortunately a legal degree does not automatically equate into smart business planning and management. To operate a business effectively, successfully, and scrupulously, it is imperative that the solo practitioner understands and applies skills that expand beyond the role as counselor. We need to be just as prepared and educated in office management, marketing, and bookkeeping as we are in case law.

Although drive, commitment, energy, and pride of ownership are of the utmost importance as a solo or small firm practitioner, as a business owner, organization and smart business planning are equally as important. Solo practitioners who only focus on honing legal skills and neglect the intricacies of operating a business will eventually be closing their doors for mismanagement. Perhaps the attorney who only wishes to dedicate time to perfecting legal skills would be better suited working at a firm so that he or she will not need to be bothered with the mundane task of running an office.

As a solo practitioner, you will need to juggle the following functions of your business:

✔ **Office Management:** this includes everything from scheduling appointments to shopping for office supplies to juggling clients and court appearances. In other words, you will be running the day-to-day operation;

✔ **Planning:** making goals and reassessing them every six months to a year to evaluate whether your practice is growing the way the way you want and what needs to be done to either get it back on track or help it progress;

✔ **Accounting:** tracking receivables and payables, reconciling financial statements, paying taxes;

✔ **Organizational Development:** examining what time-management methods work and do not work to make your practice as efficient and effective as possible;

✔ **Intellectual Development:** staying abreast of everything new and changing by attending continuing legal education seminars and annual association meetings as well as reading publications, magazines, and case law;

✔ **Marketing:** defining advertising campaigns, networking efforts, and pro bono projects to promote your visibility within both the legal and lawyering community;

✔ **Sales:** selling yourself and your skills once a potential client is sitting in your office;

✔ **Human Resources:** hiring, retaining, and terminating employees as well as defining the wages and benefits that will be offered;

✔ **Operations:** dealing with the technology that makes the business operate, and lastly;

✔ **Advocacy:** being a lawyer.

BEING YOUR OWN BOSS: THE SWEET

Your Work Is Your Own: Gone are the days of preparing a pleading for the partner's signature. As a solo, when something goes out the door, it is on your letterhead and under your signature.

Your Clients Are Your Own: You get to decide whom you do and do not represent. You get to decide what types of cases you want to take and which ones you send away.

Your Days Will Rarely Be Boring: There will always be something for you to do. Whether you are working on cases, sending out invoices, paying bills, going through mail, or making an office supply run, you will have very little down time.

You Can Make Your Own Schedule: Usually this will mean that you will over-schedule yourself but it also means that as your own boss, you can squeeze in that haircut or your daughter's soccer game. You do not need to ask permission to do any of these things.

You Reap the Benefits of Your Success: Money earned is your money earned.

You Will Feel Pride in Your Work: This will be your practice and your business and you should and will be proud each morning when you settle in at your desk, coffee in hand, to check e-mails, awaiting your day to begin.

...And the Bitter

Stress Materializes in All Shapes and Sizes: Stress comes in all forms—a missed deadline, an angry client, a printer that ran out of toner. You will lose sleep.

Taking Vacation Just Got a Little More Difficult: To go on vacation, you will need to notify clients and opposing counsel that you will be unavailable for that week. You will need to line up coverage for court appearances. You will need to make sure your billing is current. And still, when you are lounging on the beach digging your toes in the sand, your mind will wander to thoughts of what you forgot to do before you landed in paradise.

You Need to Learn How to Count: No matter how bitter the taste of reconciling your books is, you still need to do it. You need to keep track of deadlines to pay estimated taxes and then pay them. You need to make sure deposits are made as they come in and bills are paid on time.

You Will Wear Many Hats: Your new job title is: office manager, accountant, secretary, marketing director, public relations consultant, rainmaker, and of course, attorney. You must pay equal attention to each role.

Sometimes You Will Not Take Home a Paycheck: If it comes down to paying the rent for your office space or yourself, your rent gets paid and you do not.

Do Not Fear Failure

The person who does not act because he or she fears failure is also the person who caps his or her level of success. If you find yourself doubting your ability to open and operate a law practice, adjust the way you are thinking. Instead of asking: Why and how can I do this? Ask: Why not and how can I not do this? Consider what you would lose if you did not take the risk. Although the risk of opening a practice is large, so too are the rewards.

Perhaps one of the scariest prospects of self-employment is waving away a fixed salary. Equally as terrifying is borrowing against the equity in your home to finance the opening of your practice; however, opportunity will not present itself unless you take the reins and navigate your future to the path you carve. This path may be uncertain, untraveled, and unpredictable, but the greater the risk, the greater the reward and opportunity as you chart your course.

So what if you fall flat on your face? As a business owner, bumps are inevitable. As an attorney, bruises are fated. The challenge is to learn from your errors and move forward so that challenges do not anchor you to the floor when you have the potential to fly. You can recover from a failed endeavor by finding a job. If you let your fear paralyze your dreams, you will always wonder what could have been had you acted.

Jeffrey Sonnenfeld, author and professor at the Yale School of Management and founder of the non-profit Chief Executive Leadership Institute, stated in an interview with *Fortune* magazine that "Failure punctuates truly great leaders. They aren't great leaders until they've failed. Failure is the crucible, the test. They deal with it, and their confidence and capabilities are enhanced. First fight, not flight."

IT IS NOT LONELY AT THE TOP

The mainstream image of an entrepreneur is that of a highly individualistic person who works independently and without the benefit of a social network. I disagree with this premise. A smart entrepreneur recognizes the importance of building and nurturing relationships.

As an entrepreneur, you have a greater responsibility and duty to be social than if you were a rank-and-file employee at a firm. Your business depends on it. As your business grows, so too does your "circle of influence"—the people you know, whether on a personal level or as a mere acquaintance.

Undoubtedly, as a solo practitioner, you will work independently, but you will also need to surround yourself with people. Whether you turn to another attorney to brainstorm an idea or just to provide laughter and companionship over lunch, you should look to your colleagues, specifically other solo practitioners, for guidance and support.

Fostering relationships is not easy. It takes time. It takes attention. It takes action. However, it will be the single greatest activity you engage in as a business owner. Being social will assist you in all levels of your business, from managing the office to practicing law to conjuring rain. Being an entrepreneur is only lonely if you let it be.

SETTING UP SHOP

"In any enterprise, your perspiration will be inversely proportional to your preparation."
—*Scott Sorrell*

DO YOU NEED A BUSINESS PLAN?

While a passion for success and a love of the law are altruistic qualities for the new solo practitioner to possess, the less exciting planning stages will help pave the way to a solid business beginning.

While a formal business plan is not a necessity, an informal business plan can help focus your goals and what actions are needed to achieve those goals. Keep it simple.

A business plan is a forecast about where your business is going and how it will grow. At a minimum, a business plan will help you start thinking about how you can market your practice, how it will be funded, whether you wish to dedicate your practice to a specific practice area, and where you would like to see your practice in five years. It should be reviewed periodically to assess whether you are on track to achieve the goals and objectives you have set.

The following are some traditional components of a business plan. Take some time to go through each question and determine whether it can be answered at this point in your planning stages. Some answers you will know immediately while other questions make take months to answer. Do not waste your time with a formal business plan, but rather benefit from an informal business plan that will encourage you to start thinking about where you want your business to go and how to get it there.

THE EXECUTIVE SUMMARY
✔ What is your niche practice area?
✔ What reputation would you like to build around your name and services?
✔ What can you offer clients that is different from the attorney next door?

THE INDUSTRY
✔ Who are your existing clients?
✔ Who are your potential clients?
✔ What will your fees be set at?
✔ How many cases can you take on at one time?
✔ Who is the competition?
✔ How much do your competitors charge and how are they marketing themselves?

MARKETING PLAN
✔ How will you market your services?
✔ How much time and money will you allot each month to marketing efforts?
✔ How will you track marketing effectiveness?
✔ Who will design your Web site?
✔ How will you brand your practice?

MANAGEMENT AND OPERATING PLAN
✔ What are your space requirements?
✔ What billing software will you use?
✔ What accounting software will you use?
✔ What time management system will you implement?
✔ What filing system will you use?
✔ How often will you evaluate your staffing needs?
✔ What type of technology will you need?

FINANCIAL PLAN
✔ What are your start-up expenses?
✔ How will you raise capital?
✔ How will you bridge the gap in income at the outset?

CREATING A NICHE PRACTICE

Focus on what you do best and refer everything else out. The greater your reputation and experience in a given field, the shorter the path to becoming an established firm.

Traditionally, solo and small firm practices marketed their businesses as general practice firms that handled a number of matters such as divorce, bankruptcy, criminal, and personal injury. The complexity of various practice areas has convinced many solo attorneys to limit their practice. The attorney who attempts to do it all does a great disservice to his or her clients and could open the doors for a malpractice suit.

Marketing your niche practice can reach more clients when you focus your efforts on just one practice area. If you limit your practice, it is easier to stay current with the law and to become perceived as an expert in a given area. Join committees and organizations that are related to your niche practice. Participation in these groups adds to your credibility and could be a good source for referrals. Submit articles to newspapers, trade magazines, and other scholarly journals and publications. Offer to teach a seminar to particular bar sections or trade association conventions.

Fight the urge—no matter how painful—to take the case that is outside the scope of your practice (see Figure 2.1). If you turn a case down, always refer the person to another attorney who will appreciate the referral and perhaps refer something back to you. Turning down the case of an existing client is not easy but you should not make exceptions.

Niche Practice Areas

Construction Law	Copyright Law
Corporate Law	Criminal: State and Federal
Domestic Relations	Elder Law
Franchise Law	Immigration Law
Indian Tribes and Gaming Issues	Personal Injury
Probate and Estate Planning	Social Security Disability
Sports and Entertainment Law	Tax Law
Trademark and Patents	Workers' Compensation

Figure 2.1. List of the most common niche practice areas.

While offshoots of your law practice may supplement your income, their value is more often in establishing credibility and providing marketing opportunities than in generating income, as the pay is often low. Teaching as an adjunct professor at a local law school can be a rewarding experience; however, it is a demanding job that will require countless unpaid hours in preparing a curriculum and lessons. Typically, a teaching certification is not required for attorneys to hold such a position.

Your practice does not need to conform to the traditional adversarial mold of a law practice. Mediation is an alternative model in which to structure your practice. A mediator acts as an unbiased third party whose goal is to help the parties reach an agreement. While mediators may suggest options for settlement, they should not make recommendations based upon their own belief of how the matter should resolve. There are certifications and programs to train attorneys interested in mediation; however, not every state requires an attorney to receive credentials before marketing mediation services.

CAN A SOLO PRACTITIONER PRACTICE COMPLEX LITIGATION?

Fear drives most solo and small firm attorneys away from complex litigation cases. These cases consume time, money, and resources for an extended period of time and the outcome is unpredictable. So why do some solo attorneys insist on tackling cases that have been traditionally reserved for large firms with unlimited funds and support staff? For plaintiffs' attorneys, the award, if successful, could be a contingent fee far greater than what is earned by the traditional billable hour. For defense attorneys, the income stream is usually consistent, reliable, and long lasting.

With the assistance of litigation management software, solo and small firm attorneys can now manage complex cases by breaking the case down into manageable and less intimidating parts. "Brainstorming sessions can help you deal with case complexity problems," states Greg Krehel, CEO of DecisionQuest's CaseSoft division. "Early in case preparation, brainstorming helps you flesh out the critical factual disputes and set goals for discovery. As trial approaches, brainstorming helps you assess case strengths and weaknesses, develop themes, and finalize trial strategies."

Case software levels the playing field with the big firms by allowing you to do the following:

- ✔ monitor similar case filings and settlements
- ✔ evaluate venues based on attitudes of jury-eligible citizens
- ✔ sort case facts, issues, characters, and timelines
- ✔ focus on your case's strengths and weaknesses with the assistance of bench or panel studies
- ✔ profile potential jury pools
- ✔ analyze deposition transcripts
- ✔ prepare demonstrative evidence using graphs, charts, and videos
- ✔ provide post-trial analysis

The antiquated vision of large conference rooms filled with boxes of documents and scurrying support staff has been replaced with highly functional and sophisticated technology that allows a solo or small firm attorney to take on complex cases with just the click of a mouse.

What's in a Name?

Law Office of Jane A. Doe	Jane A. Doe, Attorney at Law
Doe Law Group	*Doe Law Firm*

How do you select a name that will adorn your stationery? It may sound easy, but some thought and consideration should go into this decision. The name of your law firm will go on your sign, on your Web site, and on your stationery. It will become your personal brand.

Admittedly, there is only so much creativity you can have with naming your law office. A good rule of thumb is to keep it short and sweet. It also helps if people perceive you as bigger and more established than you actually are. Think about what image is conveyed by a firm named "Law Office of Jane Doe" versus "Doe Law Firm." The second sounds more professional, bigger, and more established. Perception is everything in this profession. Likewise, you want to allow for growth by adding more attorneys without losing the brand you are trying to build. While you can remain the "Law Office of Jane Doe" and grow your firm, clients may expect you and you alone to exclusively handle their case. As "Doe Law Firm," it is the experience of the firm, not the person, necessarily, they are retaining.

How to Structure the Business

We all learned about corporations in law school but many of us probably forgot the distinctions between business entities as soon as we closed the exam blue book. One of the first decisions you will need to make as a solo practitioner is how to structure your business. There are legal and tax consequences for each business entity.

What are your choices?

✔ Sole Proprietorship
✔ General Partnership
✔ Limited Liability Company
✔ Corporation

SOLE PROPRIETORSHIP

WHAT AND HOW?

Quite simply, a sole proprietorship has one and only one owner. Not much needs to be done in order to create a sole proprietorship, because states do not require formal filing or attach any fees to such designation. However, with ease also comes risk.

TAX AND LIABILITY BENEFITS AND CONSEQUENCES

Significant liability and tax consequences fall within this designation. Because no separate entity is created from a sole proprietorship, the owner is not safe from liabilities and debts incurred. Therefore, the debts of the sole proprietorship are also the debts of the owner as the sole proprietor's personal and professional finances melt into one another.

Likewise, tax treatment of a sole proprietorship is linked to the owner's individual tax return. The sole proprietor reports business profits and losses on IRS Schedule C, which is then filed with the 1040 individual federal tax return. The owner's profits are taxed at his or her individual tax rate. Also, keep in mind, the sole proprietor would be responsible to pay self-employment tax. This tax treatment is easier than filing corporate tax returns or determining partnership income taxes.

Once you decide to join forces with another sole proprietor, a sole proprietorship is no longer a viable choice.

GENERAL PARTNERSHIP

WHAT AND HOW?

When two or more people join forces, they form a general partnership. Keep in mind that with a general partnership, each partner is bound by the actions of the other partner. Again, states do not require any formal filings or any fees to create a general partnership.

TAX AND LIABILITY BENEFITS AND CONSEQUENCES

In its simplest terms, a general partnership mimics a sole proprietorship in that the general partners are both personally responsible for all business debts and liabilities. In terms of tax treatment, although a partnership is like a sole proprietorship in that the profits and losses are carried to the partners' individual tax returns at their individual tax rates, partnership taxation is more complex. The partnership itself must file a return each year even though the entity is not paying taxes. The partners must file a K-1 (Form 1065) that will show the proportionate share of profits and losses. Every partner will pay taxes on his or her entire share of profits regardless if those profits were actually distributed to the partners or not.

LIMITED LIABILITY COMPANY

WHAT AND HOW?

An LLC is a little bit of corporation crossed with a little bit of sole proprietorship. Forming an LLC is not difficult, but it does require you to fill out a few forms to be submitted to your state's business filing office. The fee to form an LLC or a corporation is approximately $100 and the forms can be downloaded from your state government's Web site.

TAX AND LIABILITY BENEFITS AND CONSEQUENCES

By forming an LLC, an owner enjoys the protection of personal limited liability for business debts and other liabilities as well as preferred tax treatment that allows the owner (or member) to pay business taxes on the individual tax return. If there is only one member in the LLC, taxes are treated as if he or she were a sole proprietor. If there is more than one member in the LLC, taxes are treated as they would be in a general partnership.

CORPORATION

WHAT AND HOW?

A corporation is a legal entity that is separate and distinct from its owners. Much like the LLC, to form a corporation some forms need to be filed and a fee needs to be paid.

TAX AND LIABILITY BENEFITS AND CONSEQUENCES

Corporations have a right to enter into contracts, borrow money, sue and be sued, own assets, and so forth. Likewise, a corporate tax return is filed each year as it pays its own taxes on profits retained in the business.

An advantage to forming a corporation is limited liability. Shareholders, as many or as few as you want, participate in the profits through dividends, but are not liable for the debts.

How to Apply for a Federal Tax Identification Number

Online: Go to www.irs.gov. To use the online application, you must have a valid taxpayer identification number. Your Social Security number will suffice.

Telephone: You can call the Business & Specialty Tax Line at the IRS at (860)829-4933 between 7:00 a.m. to 10:00 p.m., Monday through Friday. You will immediately receive a number over the phone.

Mail: Complete Form SS-4 that can be found on www.iris.gov and mail it to: Internal Revenue Service, Attn: EIN Operation, Cincinnati, OH 45999. Processing time typically takes four weeks to receive a number.

Fax: Complete Form SS-4 and fax to (859)669-5760. Once faxed, you will receive your number within four days.

Figure 2.2. Directions on how to obtain a federal tax identification number.

APPLY FOR FEDERAL AND STATE I.D. NUMBERS

Unless you are a sole proprietor with no employees, you must apply for a federal tax identification number. See Figure 2.2 for information about how to apply for a federal tax identification number.

Also, obtain a state identification number if you have one employee or more. This can be done by submitting forms I-9 (Employee Eligibility Verification) and W-4 (Employee Withholding Allowance Certificate). See Appendix B for sample forms.

PARTNERING UP

A law partnership is a business arrangement. Deciding whether or not to partner up with somebody could be the first step to either the success or the demise of your business. A law partnership that works well can enhance the reputation and business of your practice while a mismatched law partnership could spell financial and professional calamity.

- ✔ Do not pick a law partner simply because the two of you studied well together in law school.
- ✔ Do not pick a law partner because you are friends.
- ✔ Do not pick a law partner if you have no idea how this person manages finances, because this person will have complete and unfettered access to your operating and client trust fund accounts.

As partners, each of you is equally responsible for client development, collecting fees, marketing, networking, and office management. More importantly, both of you need to bring in enough work to feed two mouths or two families. At the beginning, it may be nearly impossible to cut two adequate paychecks to each of you. As a solo practitioner with the same caseload, it would be easier to pay yourself.

As you contemplate a joint venture, consider the following:

✔ Will you focus on one niche practice or will each of you develop a different niche?
✔ Do you trust the potential partner's financial management skills?
✔ Is the potential partner organized?
✔ Do you share the same work ethic?
✔ Does the potential partner treat their current clients and staff with respect?
✔ Have you had the opportunity to view his person's written product?
✔ Can this person add value to your practice?
✔ What reputation does this person have in the legal community?
✔ Do you need this person?

As you consider joining forces with a partner, it is equally important to address what will happen if the partnership sours. Who will stay in the office space? How will clients be divided? Who will keep the equipment? Who will keep the phone and fax numbers? What will happen to the Web site?

Practicing law with a partner can be a professionally and personally fulfilling experience so long as you pick the right person as your partner. Choose wisely, if at all.

LOCATION, LOCATION, LOCATION

Where you hang your hat every morning is a decision that should be made carefully—it can dictate your future success. If your office is in a building that is difficult to find with little roadside visibility, your business could be detrimentally affected. The same can be said for a home-based office. I know an attorney who works from her house who only handles closings. She gets her work from her husband who owns a real estate company. Her practice is what she wants it to be. When she has to meet clients, she sets up meetings at her husband's office. It keeps her busy and she has no grand plans to grow her practice to a multi-attorney firm. Her practice supplements the family income, but it is not necessary to the family's financial survival; therefore, she is comfortable with the stressless ebb and flow of the workload. Solos and small firm practitioners have the advantage of mobility and flexibility thanks to technological developments. Most solo practitioners work out of their homes at one time or another, even if they have an official office location. A home office can function as an adjunct to our law offices. Therefore, some consideration should be put into making it as efficient as possible whether it is your full-time or occasional office space.

THE HOME OFFICE

Consider the following two scenarios:

Scenario 1: You roll out of bed on a Monday morning to the smell of coffee brewing. You fill your cup and settle behind your desk, still in your pajamas, and make your first call of the day. From bed to business, you have seamlessly started your day, all from the comfort of your own home.

Scenario 2: The cacophonous sound of your alarm goes off for a third time. You shuffle your feet to the kitchen to make some coffee. As you take the first sip, your son tugs at your pant leg and asks you to build a LEGO tower with him. You settle on the floor to play with your son and watch the news. You do not do any work until your son naps at noontime.

While Scenario 1 may be the ideal, Scenario 2 may be the reality if you do not structure your work day the same as you would if you were working in an office building.

You know yourself better than anyone else.

✔ Do you work well alone?
✔ Do you mind being alone for long periods of time?
✔ Are you self-motivated and self-disciplined?
✔ Have you mastered time-management skills?

If you believe you have the discipline to filter out distractions, you may have what it takes to run a productive and profitable home-based business.

In addition to evaluating yourself, you must also evaluate your home.

✔ Do you plan on having clients in your home office?
✔ Do you really want clients to know where you live?
✔ Do you have adequate parking for clients?
✔ Does your house have space to set up a separate office?
✔ Can visitors access your office without going through your entire house?
✔ Is your home easy to find?
✔ Is your home well maintained?

If you do plan on having clients visit you at your home office, your goal is to make the office as conducive as possible to productivity. It is always best to set up an office in a separate space if your home can accommodate such an arrangement; however, many offices occupy a portion of another room and that is acceptable so long as you set boundaries around that area so it does not become entangled in your personal space.

ADVANTAGES VS. DISADVANTAGES

If you are trying to grow your law practice to one in which you are a respected and recognized attorney in your chosen niche, I discourage operating solely out of your home. You will be profoundly limiting your growth potential as the disadvantages far outweigh the advantages.

ADVANTAGES OF A HOME-BASED OFFICE

LOWER OVERHEAD
This is the most significant advantage to a home-based office. Not only do you avoid expensive rent, you can take advantage of the tax write-offs for a home office.

CONVENIENCE
You can work all day in your pajamas and no one would be the wiser. However, I debated whether this would be an advantage or disadvantage because sometimes just getting up and out of the house makes me feel productive and, consequently, be productive.

DISADVANTAGES OF A HOME-BASED PRACTICE

YOU CAN NEVER LEAVE WORK AT WORK
You are never far from work; even if you close the door and call it a night, you may hear your phone ringing from your family room and may be tempted to check and see who it is. If clients know you work from home, they know they will be able to reach you day or night.

APPEARANCE
In this profession, perception is paramount to success. Potential clients may perceive you as less professional if they know you operate out of your home. They may think that you will not be taken seriously as an attorney and that you will not be able to provide the same attention to their matter as an attorney who works out of a traditional office space.

DISTRACTIONS
There will be times when laundry or making dinner might take precedence over finishing the brief that is due at the end of the week. The distractions are numerous,

and could impact your profitability.

ISOLATION

Some people work better alone, while others need to be surrounded by people to stay focused. Office sharing or executive office suites encourage a social work environment that cannot be found in a home office.

LIMITED GROWTH

A growing business requires room for staff and storage for files. If your office is based at home, the growth of your practice will be stunted at one time or another.

TIPS FOR RUNNING AN EFFECTIVE HOME OFFICE

If you decide that running your practice out of your house is the right choice for you, you need to create an environment that will allow you to operate like a business regardless of its location. The following tips will help you get organized and motivated, so you can be just as profitable at home as you would be in a formal office.

- ✔ Set up a home office, literally. You should have a room that is exclusively used for your business. Working from your kitchen table is going to encourage distractions and hinder your organization and time management.
- ✔ Get up each day like you were leaving the house. That is keep a schedule so you have set hours you are working each day in your designated office space.
- ✔ Minimize distractions. Turn the television or radio off and get a babysitter to watch the children, even if just for a few hours each day so that you can return phone calls uninterrupted.
- ✔ Set up a business e-mail that is distinct from your personal e-mail. The appearance of running a professional business is essential to obtaining and retaining clients.
- ✔ Schedule client appointments at another location, if possible. Utilize a business center; that is, temporary offices that provide traditional office space for you to work in. Typically, a business center space comes with Internet access, conference space, office equipment, and sometimes even a receptionist.
- ✔ Set boundaries. Tell your spouse and children that when your office door is closed, you are not to be disturbed. Conversely, it is easy to work twelve-hour days when work is only down the hall. Close your door at the end of the day and leave it closed until the next morning.

Although running your practice out of your home has unique challenges, it also grants you the best of both worlds. While it is not the ideal situation if you are just starting out, if done strategically, you can enjoy the benefits of being able to work flexible hours, of not having a commute, of low overhead, while also building a profitable and successful business.

EQUIPPING YOUR HOME OFFICE

Furnish and equip your home office as you would any office. You do not need to purchase the most exquisite furniture, but you do need to purchase functional furniture that will accommodate your needs. If your home office is secondary to another office, your needs are far less than if your home is your primary office. To make your office fully functional, you will need:

- ✔ **Office furniture:** Desk, chair, bookcases, storage for files. You will be limited by the size of the space in which you are setting up. Do not buy anything until youmeasure the space. I purchased a gorgeous cherry desk and credenza for my office. Then I watched the delivery men drive away with it still on the truck, because the furniture could not fit up the stairs to get to my office.
- ✔ **Telephone:** Set up a phone and fax line that is distinct from your personal phone number. It is also a good idea to have at least one rollover line that will go to voicemail rather than use call waiting if you are on the phone.
- ✔ **Computer:** While a desktop computer is less expensive, a laptop's portability allows you mobile flexibility. Get high-speed Internet service.
- ✔ **Printer/Copier/Scanner:** You can find reliable multi-function devices from manufacturers such as Canon, Brother, and HP in the range of $200 to $600. Buying a multi-function device will save considerable countertop space in your home office.
- ✔ **Fax machine:** Consider using an e-fax service that allows you to fax documents over e-mail. You save on paper, ink, and space.

Use the checklist in Appendix A to help you set up a law office whether in your home or in a separate location.

THE TRADITIONAL OFFICE LOCATION

Office space will probably be your highest overhead expense. It is important to find space that is suitable for your practice now, and in the future. Before you call a realtor, do some contemplation and research on your own.

- ✔ How much space do you need and where should you be located?
- ✔ Do you want space that will allow you to grow?
- ✔ Should you be located near the courthouse or does that not matter in the type of law you practice?
- ✔ Use the Internet to research the area in which you plan on setting up shop. Sites

such as www.epodunk.com offer valuable information about household income, education level, and average age for any particular city or town. Find an office close to home. The less time you waste driving, the more time you have to work. A good rule of thumb to consider is that you should have 400 to 600 square feet per attorney. Of that space, 150 to 200 square feet is allocated to a secretary and 100 to 200 square feet for reception, office supplies, office equipment, and file storage.

✔ Consider sharing office space with another attorney. By sharing office space, you can share the costs of a receptionist as well equipment such as a copier. However, always get your own phone lines and fax lines so if you decide to relocate later on, you can take your numbers with you. It is helpful if the attorneys you share space with practice different areas of law so that you can establish a referral network. If you are fortunate enough to join a referral circle within your office space, establish a referral fee arrangement so that you know before you receive that first referral how much you should be paying. Also, discuss whether the referral fees will be paid as legal fees are received or one fee at the conclusion of the matter.

You can enlist the help of a realtor or find a place on your own by simply checking local law publications and newspapers for available office space. Keep your eyes open as you drive around and look for signs indicating available space.

Once you locate a potential office location, consider the following:

✔ Is there enough parking for clients? Clients may avoid an area where parking is not convenient or they are subject to overtime fines.
✔ Is the office easy to find? Is it located on a main road?
✔ Is the signage visible?
✔ Is the space close to public transportation?
✔ What is included in the rent? Cleaning service? Utilities? If heat/AC is included, who controls the thermostat?
✔ Do you need to provide your own signage?
✔ Is there enough space on either side of your existing area to grow into?
✔ Is there sufficient room for support space?
✔ Is there adequate storage space for office supplies and files?
✔ Is the reception area attractive?
✔ Is there a local law library or neighboring attorneys who may allow you to use their law books for a small fee, or, preferably, at no charge?
✔ Is there a property manager?
✔ Does the space have a security system?
✔ Is the space conducive to computer network wiring without an excessive expense?

✔ Are there enough electrical outlets and phone jacks for your needs?

✔ Is there property casualty insurance or do you need to purchase your own?

✔ Is the commute easy for you?

✔ Is the space close to the courthouse or other agency offices you frequent?

✔ Is the space accessible to the handicapped or elderly if you expect them to be a substantial part of your clientele?

✔ Is the space well lit and safe after regular business hours?

As you negotiate lease arrangements with the landlord, discuss whether he or she will guarantee lower long-term rates at a competitive price. Be sure that the space is adequately equipped to accommodate a growing practice before you sign a long-term lease. Negotiating a long-term lease at a lower price is not wise if you are unable to expand your practice later on due to space limitations.

Moving is costly. Better to expand or downsize your current space than have to change your address. Discuss a right of first refusal with the landlord so that if adjoining space becomes available, you have the option to add this space to your lease. Likewise, discuss what options are available to you if you need to downsize. Your lease should also include a provision addressing sub-leasing and lease termination rights.

In the unexpected event that you need to terminate your lease, it may come with a penalty. The general rule of thumb is that the larger the space, the longer the notice period you need to give before you terminate the lease. In your lease termination options, consider what happens in the event of a merger, the death or disability of a firm member, or the landlord's inability to provide adequate expansion space.

If the space is perfect for your needs right now, but offers no expansion possibilities, try to only sign a short-term lease so that you can relocate as your firm grows. However, it is best to find space that can accommodate a growing practice as relocation is disruptive to a business.

PREPARING FOR THE WORST: INSURANCE

Disasters can surface in many different ways. A natural disaster may be just as debilitating and devastating to your business as a malpractice lawsuit. It is important to protect yourself by cushioning your business with adequate and comprehensive insurance coverage. Check with your state bar association before you purchase a policy. The association usually has a sponsored insurance company that will afford you access to a policy at a reduced rate.

PROFESSIONAL LIABILITY INSURANCE

Professional liability insurance is not required in every state; however, I recommend no matter what your state requirements may be that you obtain some level of malpractice insurance. Why?

- ✔ Professional liability insurance protects both you and clients from errors that could happen to anyone.
- ✔ Most lawyer referral services require some level of protection.
- ✔ Many corporate clients will require that their legal counsel have professional liability insurance.
- ✔ Defending a claim—regardless of whether you were at fault or not—is expensive.
- ✔ An adverse judgment could ruin you. You cannot hide behind a PC or LLC designation.
- ✔ Lawyers are responsible for their own actions and their own mistakes.
- ✔ Sometimes claims are not filed until years after an error was made, so you want to be protected from early mistakes.

If you are leaving a firm to open your own practice, you are typically still insured under your old firm's policy for work you performed while employed there. If the old firm does not continue to carry insurance, prior lawyers may no longer be insured under the policy. In this situation, you may be able to obtain coverage for work you did at a prior insured firm under a different policy. Here are some insurance tips:

- ✔ Not all insurance policies are the same.
- ✔ Deductibles may be either per claim or aggregate.
- ✔ Punitive damages are covered by some policies but not other policies.
- ✔ There may be exclusions for certain practice areas.
- ✔ Some policies give the insured control of the settlement while other policies give settlement responsibilities to non-lawyers or to lawyers employed by the insurance company.
- ✔ Some policies may not cover the grievance expense.
- ✔ Some policies exclude malpractice counterclaims in suits initiated by insureds for fees.

The cost for professional liability insurance varies. Ironically, it is often less expensive for a new lawyer to obtain coverage than it is for a seasoned lawyer to obtain coverage. If you practice part-time, the rates typically decrease also. Many insurance companies offer payment plans; payments are made over time rather than being due up front. This arrangement makes insurance affordable so cost should not deter you from obtaining professional liability insurance.

PROPERTY/CASUALTY INSURANCE

A property/casualty policy should protect against fire, flood, lightning, hail, wind, smoke damage, vandalism, theft, and sprinkler leakage. To obtain the most effective coverage, base the amount of protection on the actual replacement value of the property. For example, fire insurance policies are typically written to cover what was lost based on actual cash value of the damaged property at the time of the loss. This provision considers depreciation of property and will not provide coverage sufficient to purchase new equipment. In terms of fire insurance, rates depend on safety conditions on your area, water supply, and efficacy of firefighting equipment. All cities of 25,000 or more people are periodically evaluated and ranked according to the former standards. You can probably secure lower rates if your space has a sprinkler system, smoke detectors, accessible fire extinguishers, is free of trash, and is wired properly.

Water damage insurance is usually written as a separate policy and includes incidents related to overflow of water or steam from plumbing; heating, refrigerating, and air-conditioning systems; and rain or snow leakage. As is the case with flood insurance, water insurance premiums can be minimized by proper maintenance of building systems.

Many private insurance companies do not offer flood damage, because they can easily identify the localities that will suffer flood damage year after year. Recognizing that flood damage was devastating to people and businesses, Congress established the National Flood Insurance Program (NFIP) to address both the need for flood insurance and the need to lessen the disastrous consequences of flooding. The NFIP offers flood insurance to business owners, with the one condition that their communities adopt and enforce measures to help reduce the consequences of flooding. If you live in a community that participates in the NFIP, your building and its contents can be covered with standard flood insurance policies. You must apply for building coverage and contents coverage separately. If your business is on a low- or moderate-risk zone, your building may qualify for a low-cost preferred risk policy. Visit www.floodsmart.gov to learn more about the National Flood Insurance Program.

If you are operating out of your home, check your current homeowner's insurance policy to determine if business equipment is covered. You may need to purchase a separate policy if your current policy excludes or limits coverage for business equipment.

LIABILITY INSURANCE

Liability for mishaps that occur on your premises, through your business operations or through employees' activities, needs protection of its own kind. Do not limit your liability coverage to the value of your business, because there is no guarantee that the assets of your company will not be attached once insurance maximums are paid. You should consider setting a limit of liability for each person who might be injured on your premises, a limit for a number of people injured at one time, and a limit for property damage.

WORKERS' COMPENSATION INSURANCE

Workers' compensation programs operated by individual states protect workers in the event they sustain an injury while on the job. States have different rules about whether workers' compensation insurance is mandatory. Some states exempt employers who have a minimum number of employees.

HEALTH INSURANCE AND LIFE INSURANCE

As you contemplate whether to offer these benefits to employees, you must also consider the extent of coverage and cost. Will you ask employees to contribute to the plan or will you foot the bill entirely? You will need to decide on benefit limits, deductibles, coinsurance, and family coverage. If a health maintenance organization (HMO) plan is available, does the cost outweigh the disadvantages of such a plan? HMOs are typically cost-effective; however, many employees do not like that they are limited to choosing physicians within the plan.

DISABILITY INSURANCE

Imagine what would happen if you became temporarily disabled and unable to work. No work means no income. Disability insurance is important for the solo practitioner, but it may not be easy to obtain. Many insurance companies want to see a salary history of several years at your present employment to determine your qualification for disability insurance. However, as a new business owner, you do not have several years of earning history and, therefore, may be disqualified from coverage. Some insurance companies offer insurance to address this exact situation, but the premiums may be high and the benefits low.

MONEY MATTERS

"Only those who dare to fail greatly can ever achieve greatly."
—*Robert Francis Kennedy*

How does a person who does not even balance her checkbook manage the accounting of a business? I never sort my money in order of increasing or decreasing value. It is a game when I buy my morning coffee whether I will need to count coins to purchase it or whether I will find a dollar or two or twenty lounging at the bottom of my purse along with my son's loose Cheerios. Yet, I have managed to pull my personal money management (or mismanagement) together for the sake of my business and license.

This chapter will guide you on everything from funding your practice to managing the accounting of your business.

SHAKING THE MONEY TREE

You do not need to be rich to open your own practice. Experts will say that you should have no less than six months—although preferably a year—of living expenses saved before you open your own business. That is great advice; however, if I followed it, my office would still be an unrealized dream. If you are considering opening your own practice, you are a risk taker by nature, so getting creative with funding may send shivers down your spine but should not deter your ambitions.

None of the following suggestions are ideal and each carries with it pitfalls of varying degrees; however, if you are committed and passionate about starting your own practice and building a business, then you can replenish the funds you used to get your practice up and running. Just be sure you recognize that this is a calculated risk, but a risk nonetheless.

1. **Look to your personal savings.**

Personal savings consist of cash, stocks, bonds, a cash value insurance policy, or a retirement plan. Most insurance companies will allow you to borrow against your whole life insurance policy after three years of paying premiums. You may be able to borrow up to 90 percent of the cash value while your policy stays intact so long as you continue to pay the premium as it is due.

There is also a huge risk to raiding your retirement funds to finance your law practice. Nationally, statistics show that 80 percent of all small businesses fail within their first year. How badly do you want this? Would you rather work for somebody else, follow somebody else's rules, and make money for somebody else, or do you want to give yourself a shot at achieving your dreams? In a worst-case scenario, you need to close your doors and rebuild the funds that you used to start-up. If you are 25 years away from retirement, you have time to rebuild your wealth; however, if retirement is just around the corner, then perhaps this is not the best option.

2. **Finance with credit cards.**

How do you use your credit cards on a daily basis? You probably charge food shopping, clothing, gasoline, dining out, and other everyday necessities and non-necessities. None of these purchases fund your future. Used responsibly, a credit card can furnish and equip your business. David J. Berman, CPA and principal of Simione Consultants LLC suggests, "Most credit cards offer no interest or low interest rates for a period of time. If you utilize these offers and are diligent about paying the money back prior to the rate spiking to 15 to 20 percent, you just funded your business with 'free money.'" He cautions, "Be careful with plastic. Just because you can charge that beautiful mahogany executive desk with matching credenza, filing cabinet, and bookcase, does not mean you should."

3. **Borrow from your home.**

This is arguably the riskiest option and not for the faint of heart, but it is still an option if you have equity in your home. Banks will typically loan up to 70 to 80 percent of a home's appraised value minus the existing mortgage. You can deduct interest on your personal taxes, regardless of how the money is used. You can also take a second mortgage on your home that typically has a fixed rate, or a home equity line of credit which is usually variable based on the prime rate. You can tap into these funds as needed. The money is secured by your home so if you fall behind on payments, the bank could foreclose.

4. Ask a family member or friend.

A proud parent or relative may be amenable to throw some change into the start-up coffer; however, think about what would happen to your relationship with that person if you could not re-pay the loan. Does the loan come with strings attached? Would you be expected to provide legal services for all of your cousins if you accepted a loan from your uncle?

If you decide to turn to family or friends for assistance, put it in writing so everyone is on the same page in terms of repayment and interest rate, if any. David Berman, CPA, reminds new business owners, "Although the interest is a deductible expense for your business, it is considered income to the family member who loaned you the money. To avoid tension at the next holiday gathering make sure your relative knows this."

5. Ask a bank.

Bank loans are made as either unsecured or secured loans. An unsecured loan is one that is given without collateral. A secured loan requires the borrower to personally guarantee the loan. You may have a difficult time finding a bank that will loan for a business that is not yet established; therefore, be prepared to secure your loan with collateral such as your home. Banks typically look at your debt ratio; that is, how much debt you have compared to your income. If your debt ratio is too high, banks will not loan you money or will loan you money but at a very high interest rate.

Tips to Bridging the Gap in Income

Many who dream of going solo fail to take the leap because either they are the only source of income in the family or they do not want to sacrifice a standard of living to which they have become accustomed. You will need to decide for yourself what level of sacrifice and risk you are willing to take in order to realize your dreams. The following are ideas to help the financial transition from salaried to solo.

1. Be "Of Counsel" to your former employer.

It does not have to be all or none. If you are coming from working for another firm, approach your boss with an exit strategy. Advise him that you do not want to leave him holding your caseload and offer to continue to handle these files for an hourly rate. This "of counsel" arrangement will not make you rich, but it will keep you busy in the first few months of opening. To avoid any surprises or misunderstandings, negotiate the rate prior to engaging in an "of counsel" arrangement. Propose a rate that is half of what your former employer will receive from the client.

2. Reduce expenses.

Your fixed expenses are unwavering; however, which of your personal expenses are discretionary and which can you forego for a while? Do you have any rarely used memberships? Do you have full access to cable at home that can be reduced to basic service? Track what you spend during one month and you may notice that hundreds of dollars per month are being wasted on unnecessary luxuries.

3. Develop another income stream.

Is there something else you can do to help generate income aside from your practice? Apply to teach a course at a local community college a couple nights a week. Not only would this generate income but also potential business for years to come. Sign up for court appointments lists. While the pay is typically a fraction of your hourly rate, it is income that you otherwise would not have.

HOW MUCH MONEY DO YOU NEED TO OPEN SHOP?

You need to spend money before you start to make money. The first few months in business are the scariest because your business has not yet become profitable but you have expenses that need to be paid regardless.

Every business will have different cash needs and there is no generic method of estimating start-up costs for the solo practitioner. Many experts say you must live off of your capital for at least three months. Fixed expenses—such as rent, utilities, and advertising—do not change much from one month to the next. Start-up costs are paid once up front and include everything from stationery to Web site development to office furniture and equipment.

Set aside a small reserve for any unanticipated expenses that may arise. Signage was an expense that I never accounted for in my budget; that is, until I was told it would cost $900. As tempted as I was to break out the chisel and apply the skills learned from my sixth-grade woodshop class, I restrained myself and decided I could cut costs somewhere else.

There are always unanticipated or forgotten expenses.

DO YOU NEED A CPA?

Although you need to understand and manage your daily accounting needs, you should have a CPA periodically review your accounting records. Your accountant will also determine how much needs to be paid to estimated taxes and prepare financial reports, such as a balance sheet, income statement, and cash flow statement.

THE BALANCE SHEET

The balance sheet provides an annual financial snapshot of your business—the assets of the company minus the liabilities. The balance sheet includes:

✔ **current assets**—office furnishings, equipment, unencumbered cash in the bank, and cash due to you from clients (accounts receivable)

✔ **fixed assets**—long-term assets that are not expected to be converted to cash, such as furniture and computers

✔ **liabilities**—upcoming payments that your company will make, such as salaries and wages, payments owed for services, taxes owed, as well as long-term liabilities for debts due after at least a year, and shareholders' equity in the business. See Figure 3.1 to see how to set up a balance sheet that will display assets, liabilities, and equity.

				E	F	G	H	I	J	K	L	M	N	O
1														
2	ASSETS													
3		Current Assets												
4			Checking/Savings											
5				IOLTA Account	25,000.00									
6				Operating Account	15,250.00									
7			Total Checking/Savings		40,250.00									
8		Total Current Assets			40,250.00									
9		Fixed Assets												
10			Furniture & Fixtures		17,850.00									
11			Accumulated Depreciation		-3,570.00									
12		Total Fixed Assets			14,280.00									
13	TOTAL ASSETS				**54,530.00**									
14	LIABILITIES & EQUITY													
15		Liabilities												
16			Current Liabilities											
17				Other Current Liabilities										
18				Due to Uncle Joe	7,500.00									
19				Deferred Income	25,000.00									
20				Total Other Current Liabilities	32,500.00									
21			Total Current Liabilities		32,500.00									
22		Total Liabilities			32,500.00									
23		Equity												
24			Smith Equity		12,500.00									
25			Net Income		9,530.00									
26			Total Equity		22,030.00									
27	TOTAL LIABILITIES & EQUITY				**54,530.00**									
28														
29														
30														
31														
32														
33														

Figure 3.1. A balance sheet.

THE INCOME STATEMENT

An income (or profit and loss) statement includes your total revenue and expenses over a period of time. If you subtract your expenses from your revenue, you will be shown how much profit is left at the end. An income statement will also show accounting costs that you do not actually pay in cash (called depreciation and amortization). Depreciation is used to expense a fixed asset such as a computer over its estimated useful life. For example, if you purchased computer equipment for $6,000 and its estimated useful life is five years, you would "expense" or "depreciate" the asset over a five-year period. This creates a cash out delay in the year you bought the asset, but would only show a $1,000 expense on your income statement in year one. The remaining $4,000 would appear as an asset on your balance sheet. Accountants use depreciation schedules to determine the amounts.

Once expenses are removed, the income statement will show how much money you made before you paid taxes. After you pay taxes, you are left with your company's net income or profit. Remember, if you are a sole-member LLC, the money you take out for your own personal use is not an expense of the company.

An income statement includes:
- ✔ revenue
- ✔ expenses such as costs for supplies, rent, salaries, interest on loan payments, and insurance
- ✔ gross profit, which is your fees minus direct costs (all costs directly related to those fees)
- ✔ operating profit, which is your company's profit after deducting your operating costs from the gross profit
- ✔ net profit, which is calculated by subtracting your company's total expenses from the total revenue
- ✔ net profit before taxes, and net income minus taxes paid

Figure 3.2, on the next page, will show you how to list your income and expenses to indicate a cash flow.

STATEMENT OF CASH FLOWS

Running a business is simple math: you must bring in more money than you need to pay out. A cash flow statement is a record of all the cash that comes into and out of your business and lets you see where your cash has gone.

Cash and profit are not synonymous. While profit is the difference between income and expenses, cash flow is the difference between actual incoming cash and actual outgoing cash. As a small business, the most important aspect of cash flow management is avoiding extended cash shortages. Cash flow management is about monitoring, analyzing, and adjusting your business' cash flow. Estimate conservatively so that "in-flows" are lower and later and "out-flows" are higher and sooner. Better to have extra cash on hand than to be short.

I found the Web site www.investopedia.com useful to help understand accounting terms and how they work in relation to my business; however, it is not a substitute for using a professional accountant.

	A	B	C	D	E	F	G	H	I	J	K
1											
2		Ordinary Income/Expense									
3			Income								
4					Legal Fee Income	65,000.00					
5					Of Counsel Income	1,500.00					
6				Total Income		66,500.00					
7											
8			Direct Expense								
9					Court Fees	5,878.82					
10					Travel Expense	1,041.62					
11					Sub Contractor Fees	4,500.00					
12				Total Direct Expense		11,420.44					
13											
14			Gross Profit			55,079.56					
15			Expense								
16					Advertising and Promotion	7,073.26					
17					Attorney Occupational Tax	450.00					
18					Bank Service Charges	872.64					
19					Business Licenses and Permi	260.00					
20					Computer and Internet Expe	211.10					
21					Continuing Education	406.31					
22					Dues and Subscriptions	804.15					
23					Insurance Expense	2,470.08					
24					Medical Records Request	40.55					
25					Miscellaneous Expense	3,870.81					
26					Office Supplies	1,358.16					
27					Postage and Delivery	435.61					
28					Printing and Reproduction	1,119.77					
29					Professional Fees	3,333.58					
30					Rent Expense	16,200.00					
31					Repairs and Maintenance	166.08					
32					Research Services	207.00					
33					Telephone Expense	4,628.84					
34					Travel Expense	1,041.62					
35				Total Expense		45,549.56					
36	Net Income					9,530.00					

Figure 3.2. List of income and expenses.

WHAT KIND OF BANK ACCOUNTS DO YOU NEED?

You will need at least two bank accounts: an operating account and a trustee account. The operating account is the account from which you will pay bills, costs, and yourself. The trustee account has only one function—to hold all unearned income. Until you earn that money by providing legal services, that money is not yours to use or borrow. Attorneys get disbarred for co-mingling funds, so be meticulous, be fastidious, be rigorous in managing these accounts. Your license depends on it.

Also open a savings account for your business. Make regular deposits to this account to save money for estimated taxes or to pay expenses during a slow month.

If you have employees and payroll, you may wish to establish a payroll account. This account's sole use would be to pay payroll and payroll taxes.

ACCOUNTING SYSTEMS

Taking care of "the books" by using only physical books is antiquated and has no place in your business. Setting up a good record keeping system is essential to the financial health of your business. Many fledgling businesses fail to hire an accountant or fail to use a computerized system. This could be fatal mistake. Federal, state, and municipal tax laws impose periodic reporting requirements. Your state bar association could audit your business' books at any time. Therefore, it is important to make sure everything is in order.

There are numerous programs to choose from but the most popular is Quickbooks®, which costs approximately $200. Quickbooks allows you to produce invoices, track payments, write checks, and accept credit cards. Quicken® and Peachtree® are less expensive but essentially provide all of the same options.

Ask an accountant or someone else who is knowledgeable about the system to help you set it up. Initially, you will set up a list or chart of accounts including the following information:

✔ Equipment and fixed assets: land, buildings, furniture, and fixtures. Be sure to keep detailed records of the date of purchase of these assets and the original cost.
✔ Other assets: security deposits and prepaid insurance.
✔ Current liabilities: accounts and loans due within the current accounting year.
✔ Long-term liabilities: non-current portion of installment obligations due after the accounting year.
✔ Other liabilities, such as deferred income.
✔ Capital or ownership: accounts describing the original investments or subsequent earnings and subsequent earnings realized.
✔ Revenue by source or type.
✔ Expenses: each listed separately (marketing, rent, utilities, interest, advertising, phone, dues and subscriptions, and so on).

All transactions entered into the computer program will be validated against the chart of accounts to ensure that the account exists. You will need to input client names, vendor names, and creditors. Once you enter all expenses and receivables in the system, file paper copies of anything you receive. After you reconcile your monthly bank statements and pay the bills, file everything in accordion files.

Accrual vs. Cash-based Business

Your business income is reported as either accrual accounting or cash-based accounting.. What is the difference?

✔ **Accrual basis accounting:** based on the premise that your income is reported whether or not you received it. When you are prepaid for future services (such as a retainer fee), you may defer the reporting of the income until you earn it. Expenses are deductible in the year your liability is fixed even though payment is made in a later year.

✔ **Cash-based accounting:** cash enters and leaves your account as income and expenses. This system is much like a checkbook ledger with a running balance. You report income in the taxable year of receipt. You deduct all expenses in the taxable year in which they are paid. Income is reported if it is "constructively" received; that is, when an amount is credited to your account, subject to your control, or set apart for you and may be drawn by you at any time. For example, if you received payment for legal fees in 2008 but you did not cash them until 2009, you constructively received income in 2008 and it is taxable in 2008. Expenses paid by credit card are deducted in the year they are charged.Your tax return (as well as your financial statements) is most often based on cash basis.

While you may choose any permitted accounting method when you file your first business return, you must request IRS consent if you want to change your accounting method in another year. You may apply for permission with the IRS by filing Form 3115 within 180 days after the beginning of the tax year in which you want to make the change.

What Is a Business Expense?

Can you deduct the family vacation to Aruba if you happened to attend a professional convention while you were there? Business owners need to recognize the difference between business expenses and capital expenses. Business expenses are the cost of conducting a trade or business. These expenses are common costs of doing business and are usually tax deductible such as rent, employee payroll, and advertising.

Capital expenses are the costs of purchasing specific assets, such as property or equipment that usually have a life of a year or more and increase the quality and quantity of services. For example, purchasing computer equipment is a capital expense and does not qualify as a deductible business expense; however, you can recover the money you spent on capital expenses through depreciation, amortization, or depletion. These recovery methods allow you to deduct part of your cost each year. In this way, you are able to recover your capital expenses over time. To be deductible, a business expense must be both ordinary and necessary. An ordinary expense is one that is common and accepted in the industry. A necessary expense is one that is helpful and appropriate for your business. An expense does not have to be indispensable to be considered necessary.

If you use your car for both business and personal purposes, you must divide your expenses based on actual mileage. You can deduct actual car expenses, which include depreciation (or lease payments), gas and oil, tires, repairs, tune-ups, insurance, interest on your car loan, and registration fees. Another option: instead of determining the business portion of these actual expenses, you may be able to use the IRS standard mileage rate. Once you choose a method for deducting allowable automobile expenses (i.e., actual expenses or IRS mileage rate), you must stay with that methodology. There are numerous other costs of doing business that qualify as deductions. These include but are not limited to the following:

- ✔ Employees' pay—you can deduct the pay you give your employees for the services they perform for your business;
- ✔ Interest—business interest expense is an amount charged for the use of money you borrowed for business activities;
- ✔ Retirement plans—depending on the type you establish, retirement plans are savings plans that may offer you tax advantages to set aside money for your own and your employees' retirement;
- ✔ Rent expense—you can deduct rent as an expense only if the rent is for property you use in your trade or business. If you have or will receive equity in or title to the property, the rent is not deductible;
- ✔ Taxes—you can deduct various federal, state, local, and foreign taxes directly attributable to your trade or business as business expenses (note: this does not include income taxes);
- ✔ Insurance—you can deduct the ordinary and necessary cost of insurance as a business expense, if it is for your business;
- ✔ Business-related education—such as seminars, classes, educational tapes or CDs, and conventions.

Generally, you cannot deduct personal, living, or family expenses; however, if you used something partly for business and partly for personal purposes, you can deduct the business portion. For example, if you borrow money and use 70 percent of it for business and the other 30 percent for a family vacation, you can deduct 70 percent of the interest as a business expense. The remaining 30 percent is personal interest and is not deductible. Personal expenses, such as food, life insurance protection, your children's education, and vacation are not deductible. Be sure you have adequate supporting documentation to support your business expenses.

To deduct home expenses, you must be able to show that you use the home area exclusively and on a regular basis either as a place of business to meet or deal with clients in the normal course of your business or as your principal place of business. What does "exclusively" and "on a regular basis" mean? Exclusive use means that you use a designated area of the home solely for business purposes. The use of a home office for both business and personal activities does not satisfy the exclusive use test. A part of a room can qualify so long as you can show that it is exclusively and regularly used as the principal place of business or for seeing clients.

Even if a room is solely used for business purposes, it is not considered "on a regular basis" if it is only used occasionally. The problem arises when you have a principal place of business and you work out of your home. If your deduction is ever questioned, you must show that you have actual office facilities and show records of business visitors.

A deduction for home business may include real estate taxes, mortgage interest, utility expenses, and home insurance premiums. You cannot write off landscaping or your deck expansion as a business expense. A word of caution: home office expenses can be a "red flag" to the IRS and make you more susceptible to an audit.

For a complete list of allowed deductions, visit www.irs.gov and consult with a certified public accountant.

DEPRECIATION AND AMORTIZATION

By depreciating your assets, you can recover your capital investment in business assets. You may depreciate property so long as it is used in your business, has a determinable useful life that is longer than one year, and must be something that wears out, becomes obsolete, or loses value.

Specific depreciation rates for classes of property are provided by the IRS. The total depreciation of a given item cannot be greater than the cost of that item. Accelerated methods give you greater deductions early on and lessen in later years. However, as a new business, you will not necessarily need the greater deductions at the beginning because you can expect losses with the first couple of years.

While depreciation allows you to deduct the cost of an asset over the asset's life, amortization is a method of deducting certain capital expenses over a fixed period of time. The IRS allows you to amortize costs associated with starting a business such as the costs of creating a legal entity; getting a lease on business property; intangible assets defined in Section 197 of U.S. Internal Revenue Service Code such as business licenses, permits, patents, trademarks, trade secrets, customer loyalty (goodwill); and intangible value of physical items such as client lists and accounting and inventory records.

PAYING TAXES

Income taxes. Payroll taxes. Property taxes. The federal government probably takes the largest share of your profits through taxes. Depending on the revenue needs of your state, the state government can also dip into your profit pool. You need to be sure that your tax liabilities are calculated, documented, and met. Remember, since you will no longer receive a W-2, you will need to pay federal, state, and possibly city income taxes on your net earnings on a quarterly basis. These payments are due April 15, June 15, September 15, and January 15. You will also be responsible for self-employment tax, consisting of Medicare and Social Security.

INCOME TAX

Income tax is the net earnings of sole proprietorships and corporations. A partnership as an entity pays no income tax, but each partner pays income tax on his or her share of the income from the partnership. This is done through a Schedule K-1 that is issued to partners annually.

The due date of income depends on the business taxable year and the form of your business. The filing date may be different for state and federal returns. Note that sole member LLCs are filed on Schedule C of your personal tax return (Form 1040) rather than through a partnership tax return (Form 1065).

EMPLOYMENT TAX

If you employ staff, you must withhold and pay employment taxes. Employment taxes cover federal income tax, Social Security, and Medicare. Employment taxes must be paid no matter the type of business organization you have established. You must first obtain a federal employer identification number by filing Form SS-4. To make this task easier, turn to automated tax reporting and payroll services such as www.PayCycle.com, which is designed for small business owners and typically costs from $14.99 to $42.99 per month, depending on the level of services needed.

A consultant or contract employee is not considered an employee for employment tax purposes. Be careful that the person you claim as an independent contractor truly meets the IRS definition of an independent contractor. The IRS has established the following three-step evaluation to determine whether an individual is an independent contractor or employee:

- ✔ **Behavioral:** Does the company control or have the right to control what the worker does and how the worker does his or her job?
- ✔ **Financial:** Are the business aspects of the worker's job, such as how the worker is paid, whether expenses are reimbursed, and who provides office supplies, controlled by the payer?
- ✔ **Type of Relationship:** Are there written contracts or employee-type benefits such as pension plan, insurance, or vacation pay? Is the work performed a key aspect of the business?

Look at the entire relationship, consider the degree or extent of the right to direct and control, and document each of the factors used in coming up with the determination. If you are unsure about an individual's designation, seek guidance from the IRS by submitting Form SS-8. If you classify an employee as an independent contractor and you have no reasonable basis for doing so, you may be held liable for employment taxes for that worker. Remember to send 1099 forms to anyone you paid over $600 to who is not incorporated.

SOCIAL SECURITY AND MEDICARE TAXES

Also known as FICA, the tax for financing Social Security and Medicare programs must be withheld from employees' checks. The withholdings are typically reported to the IRS on Form 941 and are filed quarterly. The employment taxes due on employees' wages are usually paid directly to a designated depository bank. The frequency of payments depends on the size of your employment tax liabilities over a 12-month "lookback" period.

If you are a sole proprietor or a partner, your personal Social Security and Medicare liability is paid to the IRS in the form of self-employment tax, which you include along with your income tax. As a member of an LLC, you are responsible for both the employee and employer portion of FICA; however, you will receive a credit for self-employment tax on your personal tax return.

STATE UNEMPLOYMENT TAXES

Unemployment taxes are paid to state and federal governments. You must register your business with your state bureau of labor. The state assigns an identification number and an experience rate. The rate is determined by how often you and other businesses hire and fire employees. The higher your turnover, the more demand is placed on the state unemployment fund and the more you will have to pay into the fund. The longer you retain employees, the less unemployment taxes you pay. Your state will inform you when and how to deposit these monies.

FEDERAL UNEMPLOYMENT TAXES

This tax is smaller than the state unemployment tax. Federal unemployment taxes are typically less than $100. File Form 940 one month after the close of your tax year.

OTHER TAXES

Some states or municipalities tax your inventory and business property. Your state or municipality will send you the necessary forms when you register the business.

CHOOSING YOUR ACCOUNTING YEAR

Typically, income taxes are computed based on a 12-month period. If the period ends on December 31, it is called a calendar year. If it ends on the last day of any month other than December, it is called a fiscal year. A reporting period can never be longer than 12 months except when it is the year in which you start or end your business or the year in which you change your taxable year.

Businesses may not choose any fiscal year they want. It must correspond to a calendar year unless you have a good business reason for choosing otherwise. Keep in mind that if you choose a tax year that ends at a time when your cash reserves are low, you may find it difficult to pay your taxes.

10 ACCOUNTING ORGANIZATION TIPS

When it comes to managing your business finances, never guess and always seek the advice of a professional. The following are a few tips to keep in mind regarding the daily financial operation of your business:

1. Keep business and personal accounts separate.
2. Keep a separate file to store business records such as receipts and invoices.
3. Do not use a debit card to withdraw cash from your business—write checks so you can show to whom payment is made.
4. Do not use your business credit card for personal use.
5. Reconcile your books monthly to check the accuracy of your own account and that of the bank.
6. Deposit all checks and cash each day as they come in. Do not hold onto payments and retainers for one weekly deposit.
7. Pay all business bills and expenses by company check.
8. If you have to make expenditures using personal checks or credit cards, make sure you promptly submit expenses to the business for reimbursement.
9. Have a detailed chart of accounts so you can track and monitor what you are spending your money on.
10. Retain your check registers, ledgers, reconciliation statements, bank statements, and other financial documentation for seven years after the accounting year is closed.

Do not let the numbers scare you. Remember, you will have a loss at start-up because you have not brought in any profit yet. Start your business off right by enlisting the services of an accountant, reconciling your bank accounts monthly, paying your taxes on time, and evaluating your financial statements on a regular basis. When you know where your money is coming from and where it is going, you are in a better position to make intelligent business decisions.

4

FROM PIXELS TO PAPER

"If you don't know where you're going, you'll end up somewhere else."
—*Yogi Berra*

Physically setting up an office can be a daunting task. It is not difficult to do, but because there are so many choices to make, it is easy to be overwhelmed. Office furniture…computer equipment…office supplies. Where do you begin? What do you need?

I was naïve when I attempted to purchase furniture for my office. I thought it would take 30 minutes and then I could check another task off my list. Two hours later, not only did I not purchase a desk, but rather I left the store dazed and confused.

"This desk cost what? That is more than my mortgage for three months!"
"Left return? Right return? I have no idea!"
"Do I really need a chair that does all that?"

I went back to my empty office deflated but determined. I configured the layout of furniture in my mind and returned to the store. I selected a desk with a left return, matching bookcase, and leather executive chair that would fit my design vision. I felt relieved and accomplished; that is, until the delivery men told me the desk would need to be either set up in the reception area or returned because it was not going to fit up the stairs. Buy furniture—uncheck.

This chapter will guide you through the basics of what you need to set up your office.

Get organized. Get educated about your choices. Go shopping.

See Appendix A for a checklist that will help you set up your law office.

YOUR TELEPHONE NUMBER

Once you decide on an office location, immediately call the phone company and arrange for installation. Be nice to the phone company representative. This person holds the key to a memorable phone number. What the representative usually does not tell you is that the phone company reserves "special" numbers on a list that they do not draw from unless requested. This list contains the numbers that have double zeros at the end such as "555-2200." Be sure to ask for one of these numbers.

Order multiple lines. You will want a separate phone number for your fax machine and another number for your computer modem. You should also have at least two telephone numbers so that your phone never rings busy or beeps to signal call waiting. Install at least one rollover line and a voice mailbox. Schedule installation of your lines as soon as possible. If you decide to use an e-fax service, you can eliminate the cost of an extra phone line through the phone company. E-fax allows you to receive faxes directly to your e-mail in pdf files.

Ask the telephone company representative the following questions:

- ✔ What will the monthly charges be?
- ✔ What services and bundles are available? Can you bundle phone and Internet service?
- ✔ Are you in time for the next telephone book?
- ✔ What is the cost to add bold type in the white pages listing?
- ✔ What is the deadline for phone book advertising?
- ✔ What is the cost of yellow pages listings?

Phone book advertising is expensive so do not get carried away no matter how alluring it is to open the book and see a full page picture of yourself. As you will learn in Chapter 5, there are more cost-efficient and effective marketing techniques that are more worthy of your money than phone book advertising.

WHO IS ANSWERING YOUR PHONE?

Think about how your phone will be answered. If you do not have a receptionist answering your phone, you should consider a phone answering service. If you decide to have your phone go straight to voicemail, you sacrifice your credibility to existing and prospective clients. Even if you are not in the office, clients like to speak to a live person. Clients also do not like trying to navigate an automated system to find the correct voicemail box. The negative side to an answering service is that often the person answering the phone sounds bored and disinterested. The messages are typically limited to name, number, and time rather than any sort of detailed message. The phone usually rings for a long period of time before someone answers it. If you do not have someone answering your phone, then your voicemail system needs to be easy to navigate. Make sure a caller can reach your voicemail box easily and quickly. If he or she pushes the wrong button on the phone, the system should bring the caller back to the main menu rather than disconnect the call. Keep your voicemail box empty so that clients never receive a message that the mailbox is full. Make sure the message is your voice rather than a generic message. If you anticipate that you will not be able to return a phone call in a short timeframe, change your greeting to notify callers that you are in court or on vacation and when you will be able to return calls. Periodically call your office during off hours to make sure your system is easy to navigate and your message sounds clear.

ALL THINGS PAPER

Do not underestimate the power of perception. Clients expect to receive correspondence from their attorney on professional engraved letterhead. Opposing counsel might take you a little less seriously if you print letterhead from your computer. While some expenses can be mitigated, stationery is an expense that needs to be swallowed.

Your goal is to develop a defined graphic identity on all written content so that your business has a distinct visual personality. See Chapter 5 for a more in-depth discussion of creating a visual personality.

What you should purchase:

- ✔ announcements
- ✔ letterhead with a second page
- ✔ business cards
- ✔ envelopes
- ✔ pleading paper (you can avoid ordering this right away and just use plain white paper at the beginning to keep your costs down)

Most attorneys have traditional letterhead with traditional font. The printer should show you samples of other work the printer has produced. When you finally select a stationery design, make sure you proofread like you have never done before. Be sure to include your e-mail address and Web site on your letterhead.

The most important tip you can take from this section is this: Be certain your phone numbers work before having your letterhead printed. The telephone company will usually reserve numbers for you but will not guarantee those numbers until the lines are actually run into the building. It is not unheard of to reserve a phone number to find out during the installation process that the reserved number does not work or was promised to someone else who had the lines installed first. If this happens to you, you will be given a new number and no matter how much you stomp your feet and have a temper tantrum that would make any two-year-old proud, you will not get that number. If your stationery has already been printed, you will need to re-order. As much as you would like to tell the printing company that it was their mistake, this will be your expense to shoulder and an unnecessary headache; so just wait to give your printer the thumbs up until your phone lines have been installed and tested.

Announcements should include your address, phone number, Web site, and areas of practice. They should be sent to friends, family, neighbors, colleagues, acquaintances—in other words, send announcements to anyone whose address you have or whose hand you ever shook.

Your business cards should be an extension of your personality. Do not be afraid to use color, double-sided business cards that tell people what areas of law you specialize in rather than just your address and profession. When you hand someone a business card, you want that person to remember you.

Buying Office Equipment

Technology scares most people. It is smarter than us. It is quicker than us. It is more efficient than us. We need technology to operate our businesses. We need technology to stay competitive. Technology is not cheap, but it is necessary. With the countless options available, it is no wonder companies enlist the services of IT experts to set up their office systems. As a solo practitioner, your needs are simple; however, you should consult with someone who is knowledgeable about computers and technology. Do not scan the Sunday newspaper ads or visit a retail store to purchase a computer. You will later learn that you either purchased a computer that does not fit your needs or you bought one that has more bells and whistles than you will ever need. Once you are well-versed on your PC needs, either find a vendor who can help you select the right computer or order your computer online from the manufacturer to customize the machine to fit your requirements.

What Should You Consider Before Buying a Computer?

Buying a computer can be more terrifying than trying your first case if you are not equipped with the right knowledge and terminology. The following is a checklist of what you should know about buying a computer at its most basic level.

☐ STATIONARY COMPUTER V. MOBILE COMPUTER

Determine whether you would like a stationary computer (desktop PC) or a mobile computer (a laptop or a notebook). While desktops offer faster performance and expandability, laptops are more portable and flexible. If you're going mobile, consider a stationary docking station for your laptop. A desktop docking station allows you to bring your laptop home, yet when you are in the office, you still have the comfort of a full screen and keyboard on your desk. Most computers now have a video chip on the motherboard. This is cheaper than having a separate video card; however, desktop computers must dedicate about 128 MB to provide a display and when the video chip overheats or dies, you will need a new motherboard.

You can expect to spend between $600 and $1,000 for a desktop PC that includes Windows and nothing else. A laptop will cost more—$1,000 to $1,500 for one that will fit your needs.

☐ CENTRAL PROCESSING UNIT

The central processing unit (CPU) performs math calculations and functions as the "brain" of your computer. Speak to someone who knows about computers to evaluate whether you need 32 or 64 bit processing as well as the recommended processor speed (measured in gigahertz). While a dual-core or quad-core CPU may be pricey, it generates much less heat than a single-core CPU, which will enhance the reliability of your desktop PC.

☐ RANDOM ACCESS MEMORY

Random access memory (RAM) is temporary storage that provides the working space for your computer to operate. The more memory you have, the more programs you can run at once, and the better the system will perform while multitasking. For standard business applications, such as Windows XP, 512MB of memory is adequate. For more memory-intensive applications, such as Windows Vista, consider 1 GB of memory.

☐ STORAGE

The hard disk is the primary data storage location. The bigger the hard disk, the more you can store; the faster the hard disk, the quicker you can access your files. Consider the amount of data you expect the computer to store, and look for a system that supports that data with room to grow. Most computers can handle a series of drives instead of just a single drive, giving you expanded storage space as well as the ability to add more. You should have at least an 80 GB hard drive.

☐ SECURITY

Consider the importance of the data you plan to store on the system and how it will be connected to other systems that might house sensitive company information.

While every computer in your business should have anti-virus and anti-spam software installed, those systems that will hold particularly sensitive data may need to be extra-secure to better protect your company's intellectual property and networks. If you are using a wireless network, be aware that wireless networks broadcast your information out into thin air where anyone can pick up the broadcasts. Implement a wireless-specific security measure, such as data encryption to protect your information.

☐ SERVICE

Do not overlook service when you buy a computer. Splurge on the extended warranty and high level service, typically referred to as the company's gold or platinum level service. This is well worth the extra cost. Enhanced service is usually provided on-site and a response is usually quicker. Standard service is typically outsourced to other countries and on-site service is not offered. When I purchased my computer, I had numerous problems with the equipment. After several over-the-phone remedies were attempted, the company sent out a tech worker the same day and remedied the problem.

WHAT PROGRAMS DO YOU NEED FOR YOUR COMPUTER?

Selecting the appropriate software for your computer is essential to keep your business running smoothly. If your business software is too basic, too advanced, or too generic to meet your firm's needs, your productivity will suffer. At a minimum, you need the following software for your firm:

WORD PROCESSING

Microsoft Office dominates the market. This program includes Word, Excel, PowerPoint, and Outlook. Purchase this program at the same time you order your computer. If you elect to go to a retail store to purchase your computer, most computers come with Microsoft Word already installed, but you will need to purchase the remaining programs separately.

CASE MANAGEMENT SYSTEM

A case management system acts like a digital secretary and office manager combined by systematizing administrative and organizational tasks such as calendaring and contact management. Software can be integrated to allow staff to monitor all activities of a case file with a few mouse clicks. At the outset, your case management system can be simple. The likelihood of you needing a complex system that allows a multitude of users is slim, so save your money on costly systems that have been developed for larger firms. The common systems are Amicus Attorney® from Gavel & Gown Software, TimeMatters® from Data, TXT, Inc., CaseMaster® from Software Technology, Inc., and Abacus Data Systems Inc.

DOCUMENT MANAGEMENT SYSTEM

A document management system organizes your documents in an electronic file cabinet. Your documents are indexed so that you can run a search by keywords. The system can organize e-mails, scanned documents, spreadsheets, and word processing files. Worldox® from World Software caters to law firms and is moderately priced. A system at its most basic level can be purchased for as little as $400 per user with an additional fee for maintenance and support.

BILLING AND ACCOUNTING SYSTEMS

You should be doing all of your accounting on a program like Quickbooks® or Quicken®. Although some accounting systems also offer invoicing, it is usually not catered to a law firm's needs so purchase a separate billing system. See Chapter 8 for a review of various billing programs.

ANTI-VIRUS SOFTWARE

Viruses can damage or destroy your computer. Be sure to install anti-virus software on every computer in your office or subscribe to a service like McAfee. Update your anti-virus software often to protect your computer.

PROTECTING YOUR DATA

If you have not lost data yet, at some point you will if you do not back up your files. A lightning strike, power surge, or hard drive failure could erase everything. If you were diligent about making backups of your data, you can simply copy your backups onto a new computer. You can burn CDs or DVDs or use a USB thumb drive to manually copy and back up data or use a dedicated application that works with a separate hard drive.

There are companies that can remotely back up your data for as little as $25-$50 a month. The price depends on the amount of space you need on their system. Before you decide on outsourcing this vital task, make sure the company has been in business for at least five years. Ask them what would happen to their data if their company would close. Ask them how often backups are performed and what is the process to retrieve your data if you need to.

Also, be sure to purchase an electrical protection device. Skip the $15 power strip from the grocery store and invest in an uninterruptible power supply (UPS) for your primary PC. You can buy a quality surge protector for about $50 to $60.

NETWORKING COMPUTERS

If your office consists of more than just you, it might be worth considering networking your computers to allow Internet access, printers, and other computer resources to be shared by multiple people. Networking can also be used to set up company Intranet to allow various users to share software applications and files. While you can install networking, it is best to enlist the services of an IT professional.

ADDITIONAL EQUIPMENT NEEDS

PRINTER

A high-speed printer with multiple paper bins is the best choice; however, it is also the most expensive choice. A reasonable and quality alternative is a multi-function device that provides laser printing as well as scanning, copying, and faxing. To purchase a quality multi-function device, you should expect to spend between $400 and $500.

PERSONAL DIGITAL ASSISTANT (PDAs)

A PDA gives you immediate access to your calendar, contacts, Internet, and e-mails. It amazes me when I am attempting to schedule a future court date with opposing counsel and he or she needs to call into the office to confirm with the secretary that his or her schedule is clear that day. As a solo practitioner, your PDA is an extension of your office and it allows you to conduct business even when you are not sitting behind your desk.

Warning: the PDA is addictive and might cause spousal disapproval.

COPIER

A wide range of options and prices is available. You can either purchase or lease a copier. Price may depend on how many copies you anticipate making per month, and whether you want the copier to also scan documents to create electronic files. If you are sharing an office, the copier can be a shared expense.

SCANNER

The solo practitioner of today is much more mobile than the one of yesterday. Thanks to technology, attorneys can work from home and stay connected to clients. Some attorneys are even turning their practice entirely paperless, so files are always at their electronic fingertips. The scanner has made it possible to convert paper to electronic documents. Everything can be scanned from business cards to pleadings and from handwritten notes to photographs.

A sheet-fed scanner comes with an automatic document feeding (ADF) feature but can handle only flat pieces of paper or documents, while flatbed scanners can acquire images of other flat objects such as pieces of fabric. You should select a scanner that has an ADF capability and captures images at the minimum rate of ten pages per minute. As soon as documents are scanned and digitized, they become ready for electronic indexing, storage, management, and retrieval.

PHONE SYSTEMS

You can purchase phone systems through an office supply store. You do not need anything fancy at this point. Keep it simple as phone systems can be expensive and there are companies that will charge a high price to set up a system, but if your firm only consists of one or two people, this is not a necessary expense.

FURNITURE

Learn from my mistake and make sure you take measurements before you purchase furniture. I was elated when I purchased a beautiful cherry executive desk with matching bookcase only to learn that it would not make it up the stairs without taking the banisters off the wall; something I am sure my new landlord would not appreciate. After I begged the delivery men to try from every angle, I watched them take my desk away and for about a month I worked on a folding table.

You will need the following office furniture:

- ✔ comfortable office chair
- ✔ a minimum of two client chairs
- ✔ desk with work station for computer
- ✔ filing cabinets
- ✔ bookshelves
- ✔ miscellaneous office needs: pictures, plants, coat rack

Office furniture can be expensive. Before you buy new, browse for used furniture in newspaper ads or on the Internet (www.craigslist.com). A business that is liquidating its assets may be selling office furniture for a fraction of the cost.

Filing cabinets come either vertically or laterally. While a lateral cabinet is arguably more attractive than a vertical, it also takes up more space, so evaluate where the cabinet will be placed and what your space limitations are. A lateral cabinet can multi-function as another desk if you put a formica top on it. Vertical cabinets tend to be the more conventional cabinet and are more appropriate if space is an issue. Regardless of the type of cabinet you choose, be sure the drawers do not come off the track easily or that the cabinet does not tip over easily.

RESEARCH TOOLS

Most attorneys' offices are lined with expensive-looking leather-bound books;

however, most research is conducted through computerized law libraries and legal databases. Legal databases allow the user to search quickly for case law, statutes, regulations, and law review articles that may then be searched and cross-referenced, thereby speeding up the legal research process. Some state bar associations offer free legal database use with membership to the bar association. While this database is often limited, it may be just what you need initially before you can afford a more extensive research tool. As for lining your bookshelves with expensive leather-bound books, dust off your old law schoolbooks. They are leather-bound. They were expensive. They do the trick.

OFFICE SUPPLIES

Office supply stores make me giddy; however, every time I walk into one, I walk out with many things I didn't need, such as a globe that was on sale or a map of New Mexico, and without the things I actually went there for.

Use the list in Figure 4.1, on the next page, to keep you focused when you enter that paper and pen paradise.

FINAL TIPS FOR EQUIPPING YOUR OFFICE

- ✔ Think mobile. A PDA and laptop or notebook makes doing business easy from any location.
- ✔ Upgrade your computer support services AND use the service before you bang your head against your desk or throw your computer out the window.
- ✔ Back up data every day. You can do this yourself or outsource this task to an off-site data protection company. Failing to take such protective measures is risky business.
- ✔ Don't skimp on virus protection. Each computer that receives e-mails needs an anti-virus program.
- ✔ If costs are too high, consider purchasing a refurbished desktop from a computer vendor. This is a great option to get a computer with all the bells and whistles at a reduced price.
- ✔ Visit www.whatis.com for a comprehensive guide to computers and technology.
- ✔ Before you purchase software, check your hard drive capabilities and system requirements.
- ✔ Before you install business software on multiple computers, make sure it comes with a license that allows you to install it on more than one computer.
- ✔ Lastly, my favorite tip: Always measure your office space, the front door, and the stairway before you purchase a desk.

OFFICE SUPPLY CHECKLIST

Paper
- ❑ Copy Paper
- ❑ Inkjet Paper
- ❑ Colored Paper
- ❑ Stationery
- ❑ Pleading Paper
- ❑ Envelopes (custom and plain white)
- ❑ Manila Envelopes
- ❑ Pads (legal size and regular)
- ❑ Memo Pads
- ❑ Post-Its
- ❑ _____
- ❑ _____

Writing
- ❑ Rollerball Pens
- ❑ Ballpoint Pens
- ❑ Highlighters
- ❑ Correction Fluid
- ❑ _____
- ❑ _____

Labels
- ❑ Filing Labels
- ❑ Mailing Labels
- ❑ CD/DVD Labels
- ❑ Specialty Labels
- ❑ _____
- ❑ _____

Files
- ❑ File Folders
- ❑ Hanging File Folders
- ❑ Expanding Files
- ❑ _____
- ❑ _____

Misc.
- ❑ 3-Ring Binders
- ❑ Index Dividers
- ❑ Stapler
- ❑ Staples

- ❑ Tape
- ❑ Tape Dispenser
- ❑ Scissors
- ❑ Ruler
- ❑ Calculator
- ❑ Glue
- ❑ Masking Tape
- ❑ Binder Clips
- ❑ Paperclips
- ❑ Pushpins
- ❑ Rubberbands
- ❑ Flags/Tags
- ❑ _____
- ❑ _____

Computer/Printer
- ❑ CDs/DVD
- ❑ Thumb Drive
- ❑ Wireless Mouse
- ❑ Mousepad
- ❑ Printer Ink and Toner
- ❑ Fax Ink and Toner
- ❑ Copier Ink and Toner
- ❑ _____
- ❑ _____

Office Products
- ❑ Garbage Bags
- ❑ Paper Towels
- ❑ Toilet Paper
- ❑ Cleaner
- ❑ Hand Soap
- ❑ Batteries
- ❑ First Aid/Pain Reliever
- ❑ Lightbulbs
- ❑ Coffee/Tea, Water, Snacks
- ❑ _____
- ❑ _____

Figure 4.1. Office supply list.

5

DARE TO BE DIFFERENT: MARKETING YOUR PRACTICE

"Many a small thing has been made large by the right kind of advertising."
—*Mark Twain*

Everyone knows that the swoosh is Nike's® trademark logo or that the red bull's-eye symbolizes Target®. These logos have saturated the market in such a way that the company does not need to even mention its name to market its products—the symbol says it all. The American Marketing Association (AMA) defines marketing as "an activity, set of institutions, and processes for creating, communicating, delivering, and exchanging offerings that have value for customers, clients, partners, and society at large."

Branding is the foundation of marketing and is inseparable from business strategy. Branding is not about getting your target market to choose you over the competition, but it is about getting your prospects to see you as the only one that provides a solution to their problem.

"You have to build the base of your house, before you build upon it," says Steve Harris, vice president of operations for The Worx Group, an award-winning integrated communications agency (www.theworxgroup). "Building a great brand is a calculated, informed, analytical science, while promoting a great brand is a visual, emotional, intuitive science. Both need to be intertwined," says Harris. It is more than putting a label on a fancy product. The concept of branding applies to any individual or service, even lawyers, so long as there is a transaction between people.

Building and sustaining relationships and quality work are fundamental to the success of a solo practitioner; however, branding can encourage client loyalty and communicate a focused message to attract new clients. Branding does not happen overnight and it does not need to be expensive. It takes as much time to build a brand as it takes a person to build a reputation.

MARKETING STRATEGY 101

Without clients, your practice will collapse. A marketing plan is perhaps the most important aspect of your practice although it does not need to be a formal, spiral-bound plan complete with charts, diagrams, and demographic research. Simply put, the purpose of a marketing plan is to identify a client base and determine how to best generate interest in your services. Marketing can be as traditional as yellow page ads to as non-traditional as a YouTube video. As a solo practitioner, the challenge is to create a cost-effective marketing plan that gets you, your message, and your practice in front of your target clients. How is this done?

1. Create and implement a personal brand.
2. Utilize both traditional and non-traditional marketing techniques.
3. Reinforce your brand with consistency and with patience.

Do not spend thousands of dollars on traditional advertising campaigns. While advertising does build name recognition, your time and energy are better spent building your brand, your reputation, and your visibility in the community. Business that is generated from referrals tends to make better and more cooperative clients. The referred client comes into your office having already heard good things about you from a previously satisfied client. These clients will probably pay their bills on time and work with you to resolve their matter rather than against you. Now compare the referred client to the client who flipped open a phone book and blindly called you. This client has no connection to you, and most often, no idea of the value of your services but rather is looking for the "best buy." Generally, the "phone book" client will be your problem client. Therefore, your marketing efforts should be less on print advertising and more on building your reputation.

DEFINE YOUR BRAND

How is branding relevant to a solo practitioner or small firm? As a solo or small firm practitioner, you are your brand. Your name is your brand. Your reputation is your brand. Your specialty is your brand. Branding is about creating an identity for yourself in the legal marketplace, so that you are distinguishable from every other attorney in the saturated legal market.

The goal of branding is to trigger name recognition associated with a specific practice area. A generic, catch-all ad that tries to make a law firm all things to all market segments will get lost in the crowd. Select a niche practice and focus your marketing efforts on just that area of law. Your professional image is all about packaging; that is the vehicle in which you and your business are reflected to the public. The way you get your brand across is projecting your personality—WHO YOU ARE—in every aspect of your business. What your Web page looks like, the wording, the inclusion of quotes or not, graphics, the way you handle your clients, and how well you deliver promises and services should reflect your style.

Develop a defined graphic identity on all written content so that your brand has a distinct visual personality. Think about the stack of business cards you have in the top drawer of your desk. Which stand out? Which blend in with the others? Your business cards should tell potential clients that you are confident and strong, not flimsy and forgettable. Do not be afraid to use color, double-sided business cards that tell people what areas of law you specialize in rather than just your address and profession. Creating memorable business cards does not need to break your budget. Online companies like www.overnightprints.com produce quality products at a minimal cost and allow the customer to create business cards that are as creative as the individual dares.

When you hand someone a business card, you want that person to remember you.

Is your Web site professionally designed or did you use a generic template with little visual appeal? You want Internet users to click AND stay on your site because they are intrigued by both the visual display and the informational content. Use emotion. "Regardless of a person's job, social status, or personal background, people react to brands emotionally," says Donna Palomba, managing member of The Worx Group. "Build your message around emotion and storytelling to truly engage your audience," Palomba says. What do clients feel when they come to you? Distress from suffering from a traumatic accident? Anxiety from a crumbling marriage?

Clients will respond to you if you tap into their emotions.

All of these things speak volumes about your image and they either strengthen or weaken your brand. Most attorneys mistakenly discard branding as a tool for consumerism. However, whether you would like to believe it or not, clients will make assessments of your skills as an attorney based on the image of your business.

Realize Your Brand

"Like planting a tree, your brand will only take root and grow if you keep watering it consistently," says Harris of The Worx Group. Your brand should be delivered to all your potential clients, whether they found you on the Internet, read your ad in the yellow pages, or asked you for a business card in the hallway of the courthouse.

Realize and reinforce your brand by applying the visual, verbal, and written language across all communications and media. Hire a design professional to create and execute a brand that can be used across all mediums—stationery, business cards, Web site, and other promotional materials.

Contemplate the following, so you can begin to tap into your strengths and personality to define your brand:

- ✔ What is your specialization or area of expertise? A jack-of-all-trades is the master of nothing. You need to set yourself apart from the countless general practitioners out there. You want people to think of you—and only you—when their legal needs fit your area of expertise.
- ✔ What can you do to become a leader in your sphere of influence? Are there organizations or committees that you can join and take a leadership role?
- ✔ What is your personality type? Are you compassionate? Are you aggressive? Your true personality can define your personal brand.
- ✔ What differentiates you from the competition?
- ✔ What can you do to be seen and heard in your community? Visibility creates the presumption of expertise. People assume because they see a person all the time that he or she must be superior to others offering the same service.
- ✔ Do people perceive you as ethical, honest, straightforward? Your personal brand will produce better results if you are perceived in a positive way.

Creating a brand is more than just going to a printer, flipping through a sample letterhead book, and selecting a font. Brand creation should not be bifurcated from marketing strategy. It is an integrated approach designed to accentuate your presence in the legal community and more specifically, within a niche practice area. Seek professional guidance when you create your brand. Ask the person who is designing your Web site if he or she can also create a branding package. Many Web designers are also print designers. Often freelance designers will create a brand package at a fraction of the cost of a design firm. Brand creation can cost a few hundred dollars or thousands of dollars, depending on what it is you are seeking. Tell your designer that you want to keep your graphic identity simple. Do not be afraid to use color but also do not become carried away with logos and complex illustrations. You want your graphic identity to complement your personal brand, not distract from it.

Traditional vs. Non-traditional Marketing

Phone books are saturated with attorney ads. What makes your ad stand out? Your one-inch-by-one-inch, monochromatic block ad certainly will not capture attention when other firms have full-page ads and full-color ads. With print ads, it is hard to tell who sees the ad, who reads it, and who ingests it. It is nearly impossible to measure the response short of asking clients how they got your name. A complete marketing strategy utilizes a combination of both traditional and non-traditional integrated marketing, with a greater emphasis on non-traditional marketing. The purpose of non-traditional marketing is to generate client interest by attracting people's attention in a different way. "Don't stop talking. Find your voice and then speak to your audience consistently in many different ways—in print, online, and face-to-face," says Palomba of The Worx Group. When people talk about you, your services are being marketed from one consumer to another consumer. However, not all talk is good talk. The individual who acts just to create publicity may do more damage if that publicity is negative. It is impossible to undo a bad reputation, so build it carefully, slowly, and authentically.

One way to generate positive conversation is to become active in the community by sponsoring community events, donating your services to low-income clients, or hosting a Chamber of Commerce networking event that could simply mean that you provide coffee and doughnuts to the members. Building goodwill in the community is a slow process, but it is a free marketing technique that will produce long-term results if you take the time.

Other low-cost, yet effective, marketing techniques focus on your current client base rather than the clients you do not have yet. Work to keep your current clients happy. After the engagement is over, remind the client periodically of how satisfied he or she was with your services. For example, immediately send closing letters to clients when a case is resolved. Thank the client for his or her faith in your services and tell the client that it was a pleasure working with him or her. Another way to remind former clients that your firm still exists is to send firm newsletters, either in the mail or through e-mail. Ideally, a newsletter should be sent out quarterly. It can include interesting developments in the law, recent noteworthy events, or something of local community interest. Creating an attractive, easy-to-read newsletter that conforms to your firm's visual identity can easily be accomplished with desktop publishing software such as Microsoft Publisher. A newsletter should not be more than two to three pages in length and should be limited to two to three topics. Make sure the content is easy to read and not overflowing with legal jargon and legalese.

The media can be another low-cost marketing strategy. If you are fortunate enough to be called on by the media to add perspective to a story or to clarify technical legal concepts, make sure you are accurate, honest, and knowledgeable. Always assume you are "on the record" when you are speaking to a journalist or reporter. Do not be defensive. Never say "no comment" if you are unable to speak on the record, but rather simply say that it would not be appropriate for you to comment at this time. The message is the same, but the delivery is different. You can also submit guest editorials to a local newspaper, contribute regular columns for various publications, and send a news release to announce a newsworthy event.

For those brazen enough to tackle a more aggressive approach to marketing, broadcasting your services via video is an innovative and cost-efficient marketing strategy. A search of attorneys on YouTube, the popular Web site that allows anyone to broadcast a video on the Internet on anything at no cost, will bring up a spectrum of videos by attorneys trying to promote themselves in a novel marketing medium. Some of the videos are tasteful, some are meager attempts at being entertaining, and some cross the fine line of trying to generate conversation by being outright offensive. Perhaps the most effective YouTube video broadcasted "case studies" from satisfied clients speaking of their experiences with a particular firm. Obviously, the video was coming from the law firm; however, the message was coming from a consumer— one consumer speaking to another potential consumer.

Some attorneys use YouTube as a medium to not only broadcast commercials but also informational video blogs about specific areas of law. They usually post a link to their videos on their Web sites. By starring in a video blog, you are raising your visibility and positioning yourself as an authority on a specific practice area. A potential client may watch the video blog, seek further information from the attorney's Web site, and then make the final step of contacting the attorney. At that point, the client already feels as if he or she knows the attorney because the attorney has been seen and heard. You will appear as an authority, not only to potential clients, but also to other attorneys who are looking to refer cases in practice areas or jurisdiction in which they do not practice.

Non-traditional marketing provides a better way to measure the results of your marketing efforts. YouTube will track how many times people view the video. You can provide people with a URL that can be monitored to determine who came to your site from YouTube. By measuring results, you can assess which marketing methods are most effective in generating activity for your practice.

HOW TO CREATE A QUALITY YOUTUBE VIDEO

Creating a quality YouTube video is key as this medium is yet another reflection of you and your practice. If you decide to set up a camera in front of your desk and be a talking head, you risk creating a video with bad sound, bad lighting, and bad editing. Creating an effective video takes some thought, some creativity, and, of course, some money. Reflect on the following points as you contemplate whether this medium will work for you.

Develop the Concept: Look at other videos. What works? What was better left on the video camera? Think creative. Humor has its place, but be sure it is not offensive. Who is your target audience? What information do you want to provide? Where are you going to shoot the video? Your office is the obvious choice and probably the setting most used, so consider some other options.

Write a Script: Do not just get in front of the camera and start talking. You need to prepare your content for the video as much as you would prepare testimony for trial.

Think Technically: Who is going to shoot the video? Do you have the necessary equipment? Do you have a microphone to capture quality sound? Is there enough lighting at the shoot location?

Edit: Keep your video to three or four minutes. People have short attention spans. The YouTube video or video blog should drive people who watch the video to your Web site. Likewise, you should put a link on your Web site to your YouTube video. Include short segments at the beginning and end of the video to provide your company name and URL address. Edit out any unnecessary footage that does not add value to the video.

CREATING A WEB SITE THAT GETS NOTICED AND GETS RESULTS

Not all Web sites are created equal. Internet browsers have little patience and form judgments quickly about Web sites based on visual appeal and informative content. Although people still use the phone book to find attorneys, many more people are now using search engines to find attorneys. You need to create a Web site that inspires potential clients to move from a passive Internet search to the next step of placing the phone call or sending an e-mail to you.

It is easy to buy a domain name and create your own Web site using free templates, but people are savvy. They will sniff out an unprofessional Web site and quickly click out of your site onto something more appealing to the eye. You cannot cut corners in this marketing initiative.

"Your Web site is an electronic brochure that allows you to communicate who you are, what services you provide, and why a client should choose you," says Michael Manzo, owner of Zuted Design, a print and multimedia design firm (www.zuted.com). "The Web site reader is only inclined to read half of what they would read on a traditional printed page, therefore proper layout and usability of the site are the key components to great design." Launching a Web site is not complicated, but it should be a thoughtful process that you, as the owner, should actively engage in with a professional Web designer. Web site development can be broken down into five stages.

Stage 1: Register a Domain Name and Find a Hosting Service

A domain name is your actual address or URL (Uniform Resource Locator). Choose your domain name wisely. Try to make it as simple as possible and make sure that it does not inadvertently spell something you do not want it to say. If you can, try and have it incorporate some part of your practice. For example, my practice can be found at either www.bermanlawct.com or www.familylawyerct.com.

You can purchase as many domain names as you like and have each of them link to the same Web site. URL addresses are not expensive, typically costing on average $6 to $10 a year.

Purchase your URL from a company that also offers hosting packages. For example, at www.godaddy.com, a company that provides more than just controversial commercials, you can purchase your URL and choose a hosting package that meets the needs of your company. You may have a free e-mail address from hotmail or another similar provider for personal e-mail; however, I suggest you set up an e-mail account that coordinates with your domain name for your business. It is much more professional, and frankly, appearances are important in this industry. Most packages offer a couple of free e-mail addresses when you purchase the most basic hosting package. However, if you need e-mail addresses for staff, you may need to purchase a package that offers additional addresses.

The most basic of hosting packages will serve the practitioner who only wishes to launch an informational site. Hosting packages are not expensive, costing approximately $4 per month for a basic package.

While some services offer Web hosting for free, it usually encompasses advertising on your Web site which is not only distracting, but also is unprofessional.

Stage 2: Find a Web Design Professional

Hiring the right Web designer for your practice will require some research. The cost to design a Web site is an investment in your business. While the prices can range from as much as $5,000 to design a Web site to a more reasonable $750, not all designers are created equal. Do not assume that the more you pay, the better your site will be. Look for an independent designer rather than a "design house" or design agency. Independent designers charge less because they typically have less overhead. Sometimes large design agencies filter their work to freelance designers and then slap a hefty fee on the invoice under the auspices of doing the work themselves. Many independent or freelance designers charge per page, averaging about $100 per page, and flash development costing on average $75 per hour.

How do you find a Web designer? Surf the Web for other attorney Web pages. The designer's name is usually at the bottom of a Web page. Likewise, do not underestimate word-of-mouth. Who did your colleagues use to design their Web sites? Contact your local Chamber of Commerce and ask if they have any members who are Web page designers. Chances are you will be given a list of them. Now call each one and start asking questions such as:

- Do you use templates or produce custom designs? Anyone can purchase a template and fill in blanks.
- Does the price include images or will you need to purchase these images separately?
- Is there an additional charge for updates and revisions after the site is launched?
- Can the designer provide you with the URL of other sites he or she has designed?
- What does the price to design a Web site include?

STAGE 3: DESIGN A CONTENT-RICH AND USER-FRIENDLY WEB SITE

Content is key. A designer can lay out a beautiful site with colorful pictures, but if the content is lacking, so is the quality of your site. Each page is not just one bit of information but rather can be multiple sources leading to additional information, additional links, and additional opportunities to draw clients in.

Be sure to include the following information in your Web site:

✔ **Your biography**
✔ **Practice areas**
✔ **Content about each of your practice areas**
✔ **Question and answer page addressing common client concerns**
✔ **Contact information**
✔ **What towns and cities you serve**
✔ **Legal disclaimer, such as:**

> There is no attorney/client relationship created by accessing this Web site or by communication with this firm through e-mail. This Web site is intended for information purposes only and it is not intended to offer legal advice. Every case is highly fact-specific. The outcome of a case will vary depending on the unique facts and legal issues involved. Please do not make decisions about legal matters without having a direct, one-on-one consultation with an attorney that knows all the relevant facts of your case.

"Produce your own content…and proofread, proofread, proofread," says Manzo. Do not instruct your designer to cut and paste content from other sites or print materials. Print out all of your content in a Word document and then provide it to your designer only after you are confident it does not contain any typographical errors. You may be charged to capitalize a letter after your Web site is launched or if you did not proofread thoroughly prior to submitting to your designer. Your Web designer is not an editor.

"Take a newspaper approach to your information layout," suggests Manzo, "so that content is provided in small, neat columns of information that are easy to read. Readers will quickly lose interest if the content is laid out in long wide paragraphs." Do not underestimate the importance of visual impact of layout.

The images you use on your Web site are equally as important as the content. Be proactive about what images you would like to see on your Web page. Go to www.istockphoto.com to select from thousands of images. If you allow your Web designer to select images for you and you decide you do not like the images that were selected, you may be charged to purchase additional images.

"Stay simple," says Manzo. "One should appreciate the eye fatigue of a Web user and avoid using annoying graphics that are likely to turn a reader away from the site rather than draw them further into your site. The cleaner the design, the more likely a user will stop."

Your Web site should be easy to navigate so that a user can easily go back to your home page. Make sure the navigation tools are defined and are the same on each page of your Web site. Hyperlinks should be incorporated into each page. These are key words throughout your Web page that can be clicked on to bring a user to another page.

"Trust your designer. Designers know what works and what doesn't," says Manzo. "If your designer is trying to steer you away from a certain design that you are insisting upon, ask them why. What you think might be interesting, may not transfer well on a Web site."

STAGE 4: OPTIMIZE SEARCH ENGINE QUERIES

Although the cost to purchase a domain name and host are relatively low, the cost to make sure your Web site is seen comes with a hefty price tag. Ask your designer to add "meta tags" for key words and descriptions for whatever services you provide (i.e., divorce, family law, custody, bankruptcy). Meta tags provide the search engine "spiders" (that is what catalogues Web sites) to get a summary of your Web site and help position your site further up on the list.

Ad words can be purchased from search engine such as Google Ad Words. You provide the key words such as "divorce attorney," "custody," "bankruptcy." Then you decide how much money you would like to dedicate each month to this service. You will get charged every time your URL is clicked on. When you reach your maximum allowable clicks per month, your URL will cease appearing as a banner ad or sponsored link.

Similarly, some services charge a flat monthly fee and guarantee a certain amount of clicks per month. For example, $100 per month from one service will guarantee 30 clicks per month on your URL. Repeat clicks from the same source are not counted towards the 30-click total that prevents someone from clicking on your URL 30 times to exhaust your monthly limit.

You can also advertise your practice and promote your Web site for free by posting an ad on www.craigslist.com. Simply create a post that tells consumers what services you provide and direct them to your Web site for more information. If you employ this promotional tactic, you should post a new ad every day so it remains on the first page of services for the geographical location in which you posted.

Another cost efficient—yet time-consuming—promotional tool is to become active in pertinent discussion forums and blogs. If you post thought-provoking comments on forum discussion sites, you can drive potential clients back to your Web site.

A note of caution: Be authentic and not just a salesperson. People can sniff out when someone's sole purpose of a comment is self-promotion. If you add valuable insight on a topic in which you have pertinent knowledge, the reader will realize that you may have other valuable things to say and click on your URL link to read further. By linking back to your site from another site that is already generating traffic, you will help your URL climb to the top of the search engines.

STAGE 5: UPDATE YOUR INFO REGULARLY

You want to keep your Web site current with content that will draw people back to your site for more information. There are two ways to update your Web site: have someone do it for you or do it yourself. Some developers will charge a minimal monthly fee to keep them on retainer. Other developers will charge a fee per change such as $25 every time you ask the designer to revise the content.

On the other hand, you can purchase a program like Adobe Contributor® for about $100 that allows you to make the changes yourself as frequently as you like. The program is easy to use even for less computer-savvy individuals.

THE "DON'T" LIST

Overzealous Web design can result in slow traffic and lost business leads, so as you configure your Web site, there are some mistakes you should avoid.

✔ **Don't Put Your Photo on the Home Page.**
Your Web site should be about your firm and the services you provide, not about what you look like. Save the photo for the "About Us" link and keep the home page direct and professional.

✔ **Don't Get Carried Away.**
Just because you can use a dizziness-inducing flash home page does not mean you should. When you exercise excess visual and audio features, your site distracts from the services you are trying to promote. Furthermore, flashy intros with music can take a long time to download and cause impatient Web surfers to flee.

✔ **Don't Have too Many Menu Options.**
Keep the site structure simple and easy to navigate. There is no limit to the amount of information you can put on your site. Too many options create confusion and user frustration. You don't want people getting lost on your Web site. Make it easy to use.

✔ **Don't Use Legal Lingo.**
Your Web site should inform potential clients of what you do and why they may need your services. Try to connect with your target audience. Your clients are looking at your site because they have legal needs. Tap into what they need and provide it to them in easy-to-read content. If your site reads like a legal brief, you will lose readers quickly. Keep your content simple and clear in language that people can understand without having a legal degree.

✔ **Don't Include Client Testimonials.**
Client testimonials serve no purpose on your Web site. Results you obtained for one client cannot be guaranteed to another. Furthermore, disclosure of client names raises ethical considerations.

✔ **Don't Become Complacent.**
Keep your information fresh, current, and accurate. Review the content on your site on a regular basis and revise it as needed. Make sure the links on your site are still active.

✔ **Don't Fall Prey to Predators.**
People get scared of technology and design agencies know this and take advantage of this. Web design can be a one-shot expense. You do not need a company to monitor your Web site and you certainly do not need to engage in a long-term contract.

BLOGGING BASICS

Gone are the childhood days of writing your personal thoughts in a locked diary that was kept hidden from a prying sibling. Now it is common for people to write Web journals, or blogs, for all to see. What some people do not realize is that blogging can be a marketing tool for the professional also. Most attorneys do not blog and there is little competition out there, but a blog can enhance your reputation as a reliable and trusted authority on a particular topic.

The goal of a blog is to start conversations. A blog should educate, inform, and stir debate. You want to lure people back to your blog to keep talking. Create a blog about a specific practice area and keep it active, so people keep coming back. Dedicate one hour–at most, a week–to updating your blog. Once you get the hang of it, you should be able to update your blog in 20 to 30 minutes.

You can set up a blog at no cost through www.wordpress.com. Pick a name that tells readers what the blog is about before they even read a page. While I do not recommend using free templates to set up your Web page, you should initially use a free template to set up your blog. Because free templates are available to anyone, chances are someone else's blog may look the same as yours so you run the risk of not being memorable. A Web designer can create a custom blog that corresponds with your personal brand so that your blog is memorable; however, a custom blog comes with a price tag. Some designers may charge as little as $300 to as much as $5,000 to design a blog, so only invest your resources if you are certain that you are a dedicated blogger.

Outsourcing may be a desirable solution for someone who wishes to set up a blog, but does not want to have the tedious task of getting it seen. There are companies whose sole purpose is to set up, host, and market your blog. Before you decide to outsource this task, do your research because cost varies from one company to another. I strongly recommend G2WebMedia (www.g2webmedia.com), a company that customizes blog design, educates, supports, and hosts sites. This company typically charges $2,000 for custom design and as little as $45 per month to support and host the site. Furthermore, G2WebMedia is platformed on the gold standard for the industry—WordPress. WordPress has a templating system that can be rearranged and edited for more advanced customizations to allow your blog to grow as your practice grows.

LexBlog is another option that carries a higher price tag. They too create a customized blog, host the blog, perform search engine optimization to increase your blog's ranking, teach you how to blog, and promote your site by registering you with blog directories. However, LexBlog typically charges $2,100 to $2,500 to design a site and as much as $200 per month for support services. LexBlog is platformed on Moveable Type, which is less desirable than WordPress. Regardless, all content should come from you in your voice. Do not allow a company to provide content. It will appear to clients as it is—unauthentic.

Link your blog back to your Web site and start writing and keep writing. See Figure 5.1 for a list of blogs and the URLs they link to. Content should be a priority in blogging; however, there are many blogs that contain great writing that languish at the bottom of search engines that deserve to be read. So while your focus as a blogger should be on content, there are a few things you can do to help your blog get seen.

BLOG NAME	URL
Build a Solo Practice, LLC	http://buildasolopractice.com
My Shingle	www.myshingle.com
The Start Up Lawyer	www.thestartuplawyer.com
Blog for Profit	www.blogforprofit.com
Aspiring Solo	www.aspiringsolo.blogspot.com
Practical Lawyering	www.practicallawyering.com
Above the Law	www.abovethelaw.com
Home Office Lawyer	www.gdgrifflaw.typepad.com/home_office_lawyer
Inquiry Into Economics of Law Firms	www.adamsmithesq.com/blog
JD Bliss	www.jdblissblog.com
Legal Sanity	www.legalsanity.com
Lean and Mean Litigation Blog	www.leanlitigation.typepad.com
The Non Billable Hour	www.thenonbillablehour.typepad.com
Solo Practice University	http://solopracticeuniversity.com

Figure 5.1. A list of blogs and the URLs to which they link.

Links that drive traffic to your Web site are arguably the most effective way of climbing search engines results pages. Every link to your site is seen by the search engines as being a vote of confidence in your site. The best way to encourage others to put a link to your site onto their site is to write quality content that people will want to read. Likewise, by commenting on other blogs about relevant topics, you can inadvertently direct readers to your site. Another way to generate traffic to your site is to submit your blog link to directories. Many directories allow you to submit your link at no charge.

As you blog, keep the following in mind to help promote your blog within the search engine rankings:

Keyword Rich Content: Think about under what topic you would like readers to find your blog. What are the keywords that appear in your article? Now use these words in the title of your article and in the body of your article. Use them as much as you can without it becoming obvious and annoying to the reader.

Pick a Niche: You will rank higher among search engines if you have substantial material on similar topics and themes compared to creating a general blog. For example, if your practice is a general practice, for purposes of the blog, pick only one topic and blog on just that topic such as family law rather than a blog that one week contains an article on alimony and the next week contains an article on deposing an independent medical examiner in a workers' compensation case. The search engines may start to view your blog as an authority on a specific topic if you build a blog with page after page of content on the same theme.

Keep It Simple: Search engines like easy-to-navigate sites that do not have too much flash and visual graphics. Also, keep your links updated so they are active.

Interlink Your Site: Make sure every page links back to your main page and any other important pages on your site. If you're writing on a topic you have previously written about, link to what you wrote before or use a "other relevant posts" feature at the base of your article.

Update, Update, Update: The more you update your content, the higher the ranking among the search engines. Schedule blogging time into your calendar so that the content stays fresh. You should update your blog once or twice a week.

Link to Other Relevant Blogs: If there is another site that you believe is relevant and useful, provide the link on your blog.

Keep Your Posts Concise and Focused: The more specific a topic is in a post, the better the search engines will rank it. Plus, readers have short attention spans so write a concise piece, 250 to 500 words, that is informative and to the point. If you have a lot to say on one topic, break it up into sub-topics.

Be Authentic: Write in your own voice. Do not attempt to sell your services through your blog. Readers are savvy and will flee if they feel like they are being pitched to.

Build a Quality, Comprehensive Blog: Bigger sites tend to rank better than smaller sites; however, do not just fill your pages with useless content. Write something worth reading. It will take time to build a site but so long as you include unique, accurate, and thought-provoking, information on your site, you are on your way to becoming a blogging authority.

While many attorneys would be happy to turn back the clock to the time when they were not permitted to advertise, survival dictates that our services must be promoted like those of any other business owner and salesperson. While marketing could cost thousands of dollars, the simplest efforts do not require money nor any magic tricks. Take care of your clients and they will take care of you through referrals and words of praise to their co-workers, family members, and friends. Make it easy for those people to find you on the Internet. Once you connect with clients, stay connected though newsletters, blogs, and frequent correspondence. Be visible in your community. Perhaps, most importantly, your business will live and die by your reputation so focus less on expensive full-page phone book ads and more on building a personal, positive reputation within your community.

6

ALWAYS TALK TO STRANGERS: NETWORKING TO MAKE RAIN

"He who has a thousand friends, has not a friend to spare, while he who has one enemy shall meet him everywhere."
—Ralph Waldo Emerson

Your success as a solo practitioner and business owner will depend more on than just what you know; it will depend on who you know. Although networking is similar to marketing, it is different in that it focuses on building and maintaining relationships with people from all facets of your life. The purpose behind networking is to keep yourself in the forefront in the minds of clients, mentors, peers, and other networking contacts so that they think of you—and only you—when they need an attorney. Everyone has a vast network of contacts; however, if you do not stay in touch, the relationship atrophies. Networking is a two-way street of giving and receiving. You must accept support as well as offer support, and by doing this, you strengthen relationships. In the same respect, you are the center of your network, which means you are the central link to everyone else in your networking circle.

Building and sustaining relationships and quality work are fundamental to the success of a solo practitioner; however, branding can encourage client loyalty and communicate a focused message to attract new clients. Branding does not happen overnight and it does not need to be expensive. It takes as much time to build a brand as it takes a person to build a reputation.

NETWORKING TO MAKE RAIN

Networking is not as simple as just attending a professional function. Habit dictates most people's behavior when they attend these events. It is easier to converse with people you already know than it is to start up a conversation with a stranger. To network effectively, not only must you actively engage in conversation, but just as importantly, you must follow up with the people you meet at these events.

"Think relationships, not transactions. Think conversation, not sales pitches," teaches Kathy McAfee, president of Kmc Brand Innovation LLC (www.marketing-motivator.net). As a marketing coach and consultant, McAfee motivates professionals to become recognized leaders in their field by mastering the art of influential communications. "If you want to grow your business and career through referrals and recommendations, networking must be one of your key strategies now and for the rest of your life. Your output is directly proportional to your input. If your input includes your full energy, then your output may be referrals, recommendations, leads, friendships, reputation, and new opportunity. Remember, the true spirit of networking is helping others and asking for help."

Networking is not a sales activity, but rather it is an opportunity to build relationships one small step at a time, so that you can get to know people and learn how you can be of service and value to one another. People do not like to be solicited. Focus on the person, not the service you are selling.

Where does one go to network? Networking can be done in both formal and informal settings. Belonging to organized groups and clubs, such as those listed below, can provide regular opportunities for you to participate in formal networking events.

- ✔ local Chamber of Commerce meetings
- ✔ bar association events
- ✔ alumni associations
- ✔ professional associations
- ✔ neighborhood groups
- ✔ civic organizations

However, merely belonging to one of these associations is not the same as being visible within the group. Showing up to events and being active within the organization creates visibility and furthers your networking goals.

Informal settings can provide equally rich networking opportunities for you and your growing practice. Remember to tap into your own personal interests as potential networking sources. For example, a book club, a cycling group, and a play date group can all be networking venues. Networking can also be as informal and simple as talking to someone behind you in line at the supermarket. With practice, repetition, and consistency, networking should become part of your life as a way you interact and relate to people. Keith Ferrazzi, author of *Never Eat Alone* (Random House, Inc., 2005) and CEO of Ferrazzi Greenlight, a marketing and sales consulting firm, advocates:

> For me, the best thing about a relationship-driven career is that it isn't a career at all. It's a way of living. Several years ago, I started to realize that connecting was actually a way of seeing the world. When I thought and behaved in that way, dividing my life between professional and personal spheres no longer made sense. I realized that what made you successful in both worlds were other people and the way you related to them. Whether those people were family people, work people, or friend people, real connecting insists that you bring the same values to every relationship. As a result, I no longer needed to make a distinction between my career happiness and life happiness—they were both pieces of me. My life.

The purpose of successful networking is to integrate it into your life so that it is no longer a separate business task, but rather, it becomes part of who you are and how you function as a business owner and entrepreneur.

NETWORKING: THE PROCESS

BEFORE YOU ATTEND AN EVENT...

LESSON #1: GO PREPARED

"Attention everyone. We are going to start this meeting by going around the room and having everyone introduce themselves to the group by telling us your name and what you do."

Panic sets in at this point. Name. Check. I know that. What I do? Ok, I'm an attorney, but what can I say about myself that is going to make people remember me?

"Why don't we start on this side of the room."

One, two, three, four....only four people away before I need to tell everyone I am just another attorney. Why didn't anyone tell me I would need to introduce myself to a room full of people?

When you attend formal networking functions, be prepared to give a thirty-second business pitch of who you are and what you do. "Most people spend their precious thirty seconds going on in boring detail about what they do. They forget to reveal who they are. The whole point of giving a thirty-second introduction is to position yourself in such a way that attracts the right kind of people to you. In this way, you can find out who you can help and who can help you. Remember, it's not a transaction or a close, but rather, a beginning of a conversation that can potentially lead to a new relationship," coaches McAfee.

Your thirty-second pitch should pass the MR. ABE test:

M—Memorable (Something has to "stick" in their mind after you stop talking.)

R—Relatable (You must connect to what the other person or people in the room care about.)

A—Authentic (What you say must be true about you.)

B—Believable (They must see it as plausible as coming from you.)

E—Engaging (It's all about energy. Dial it up!)

If you take a few moments and think about what you want people to remember about you, then you will reduce the chances of sounding like "blah, blah, blah."

Likewise, focus on one practice area. If you are a general practitioner and you tell the room that, you probably won't be remembered. However, if you tell the room you help people navigate through the most difficult time of their lives after they suffer from an injury or as they steer through the anxiety and emotions of family court, then you are creating a visual image of who you are as a person rather than just what you do as a job.

Lastly, do not forget to bring an ample supply of business cards with you. You do not want to scribble your name and number on a napkin to hand to a new contact. Your "napkin card" will likely end up being used as a coaster for somebody's drink before the event is over. It is unprofessional and makes you forgettable.

DURING THE EVENT....

LESSON #2: BUILD RAPPORT

How often do you engage in conversation with someone and instead of focusing on what they are saying, you are focused on your own thoughts? Networking depends on building rapport with somebody. To build rapport, you first must be fully present. That means, turn off your cell phone, control your shifting eyes that want to scan the room, and give your total attention to the other person.

Building rapport with the person you are speaking with will make the person feel as if he or she has connected with you because when people are like each other, they like each other. If you are looking for it, you can easily focus on commonalities with the other person rather than differences.

Tad James, MS, PhD, master trainer of Neuro Linguistic Programming, says, "No matter what you do, the ability to develop and maintain rapport with people of varying backgrounds will allow you to get what you want."

Rapid rapport techniques are founded on the science of kinesics and communication. Studies done in the 1970s by UCLA Professor Albert Mehrabian and Robert

Birdwhistle of the University of Pennsylvania led to the development of a model of communication that is still relevant today. Their communication model suggests that it's not just what you say, but how you say it (or don't say it) that creates the meaning of your face-to-face communication.

> **Verbal**—7% of meaning is in words that are spoken
> **Vocal** —38% of meaning is the tonality (the way that the words are said)
> **Visual**—55% of meaning is physiology (facial expression and body language)

Building rapport requires you to pay less attention to your own thoughts, and more attention to the other person. How do you do this? To build rapport on the unconscious level with the other person, subtly mirror and match the other person's physiology (i.e., body language, stance, tilt of head), tonality of voice (i.e., speed, loudness, pitch, quality of voice), and language patterns. By pacing the other person's energy levels, you create a feeling of comfort for both parties. This is helpful when you first meet with a potential new client also. For example, the next time you meet with a potential networking contact or meet with a new client, try mirroring and matching them in these ways:

- ✔ **Posture:** Does the person sit forward or lean back in the chair? Does the person slouch? Is his head tilted? Are his arms crossed or is he speaking with his hands? As naturally and authentically as you can, assume a similar position and do what he does. When it's your turn to speak, match or mirror his hand gestures.
- ✔ **Tonality:** If the person is speaking quickly and loudly, you do the same. On the other hand, if the person is speaking slowly and quietly, you match this cadence.
- ✔ **Language:** Listen for the types of words the person is using and align with his or her preferred "channel" of language. For example, if you hear the other person using visual words and predicates such as "I see what you're saying" or "Show me what that would look like," then you will want to respond using visual-type words as well, such as see, look, show, illustrate, imagine, visualize. By being flexible in how you speak, you reduce resistance and increase rapport. Remember, there are no resistant clients, only inflexible communicators.
- ✔ Furthermore, one of the easiest and quickest ways to let an individual know you are listening is to use the person's name. People respond to the sound of their names so when you meet someone, sprinkle it into the conversation and watch how the interaction is enhanced because the person feels like you are paying attention.
- ✔ When you are in rapport with another person, opportunities open up wide. Resistance is minimized, connective energy is increased. Rapport techniques

take practice, but the outcome is well worth what you put into it.

THE EVENT IS OVER. NOW WHAT?

After you leave the event, immediately jot down a few notes about the person on the back of his or her business card such as when and where you met, key personal information, and any connections promised. Do this while your conversations are fresh.

Update your database with contact details as soon as possible after the event. Do not procrastinate and let the business cards pile up.

LESSON #3: FOLLOW-UP

This is the most important part of this chapter. Without follow-up, you will quickly be forgotten. Follow-up does not happen just once. It needs to occur frequently so that the person remembers you when they need your services or hear of someone else who could use your services.

Although there is no substitute for a follow-up phone call, most people do not have time to place the call, take the call, or they simply want to avoid an awkward exchange over the phone. The key is finding a method that works for you and being consistent with its execution.

My preferred follow-up method is periodically sending personalized cards. I use a system called Send Out Cards, which makes follow-up quick, easy, and memorable. There is something more personal and memorable about receiving a card in the mail than an e-mail. People get inundated with hundreds of e-mail messages on a daily basis, but they rarely receive a personal card or note in the mail anymore. Send Out Cards is a service that allows you to quickly select a card design, write a message, type in the mailing address and the system prints it, stamps it, and mails it in an envelope that looks like someone hand wrote. You can input your own handwriting font and signature to personalize the card even more. Every time you send out a card, the system stores the name and mailing address to easily build a database of your contacts over time.

At my one-year business anniversary, I sent out cards to all those who referred cases to me. I also try to send out cards following an initial consultation if I am interested in taking the case or after I close a case to thank the client for the business. It takes only a few minutes to pick a card, enter the address, message, and click "send." The feedback has been resounding. People who have received these cards have commented that it made the difference in choosing an attorney because they felt like if I took the time to send them the card and a personal note, then I would take the time to listen to them as a client. To send out a free card on me, go to www.sendoutcards.com/solopractice.

The key to follow-up is picking a method that works for you to stay connected, and doing it. McAfee employs the 50-5-10-2 networking strategy she learned from tennis pro and friend, Angelo Rossetti, who learned it from a gentleman named Ernie at a networking event. The concept behind the 50-5-10-2 method is leveraging the people who are already in your rolodex, BlackBerry,® palm pilot, and contact lists. Leveraging your current network is the key to building your future network.

1. Identify 50 people with whom you want to cultivate long-term relationships. These people should be from different spheres of your life, including work, social, community, volunteer, past, hobbies, and so on. Create a diversified list of people.
2. Make contact with each of these people every five weeks, but not all at once.
3. Contact 10 people each week, which equals two people each day of the five-day work week.

Once your list is made, how do you contact these people? Perhaps you can call one person while driving to or from work. Send a personal postcard or card or use a service like Send Out Cards.

How to Successfully Execute the 50-5-10-2 Strategy

50 = Identify your top 50 networking contacts. Note: they should represent people from several types of networks: personal, professional, work, social, community, family, hobbies, etc.

5 = Set a goal to connect with each person once every five weeks. You can do this by phone, letters, face-to-face visits, etc. The content can vary widely. Call on their birthdays, request input, share news with them, send an article of mutual interest, or simply just say, "Hello, I was thinking about you. How are things going?"

10 = Reach out to 10 people every week.

2 = This breaks down to 2 people each weekday. Schedule it. Program their contact details into your phone or PDA. Enroll in programs like www.sendoutcards.com to make it easy to send personal cards or postcards. The key is to create a systematic process to support your efforts. Get disciplined to network with your top contacts on a daily basis.

Get Motivated >>> Get Connected >>> Go Forward

Figure 6.1 will give you an idea how to use the 50-5-10-2 strategy.

NO TIME IS NO EXCUSE

Between work, family, and other daily obligations, many business professionals do not make the time to keep their business and personal networks alive and thriving. They allow important relationships to fade away and fail to make new connections. As a solo practitioner, it is easy to develop tunnel vision, rarely leaving the office or reaching out to anyone beyond your immediate colleagues.

"Networking is all about building and sustaining mutually beneficial relationships," writes Diane Darling in her book entitled *The Networking Survival Guide* (McGraw-Hill, 2003). McAfee expands on that sentiment and adds "Networking is all about building and sustaining mutually beneficial relationships before you need them." Networking happens at home, at work and in our communities. Networking is a key strategy for managing successful careers, creating life-long friendships and earning a reputation as a valuable resource to others. To make this happen, you must approach networking as a lifetime endeavor—not a hit-and-miss proposition. You must embrace the true spirit of networking—helping others and asking for help. You must actively practice networking every day.

TOP 10 NETWORKING TIPS

Networking takes effort. It does not happen by accident. It is the result of time, energy, and a commitment to build relationships in order to build your business. Rainmaking can occur through networking if you incorporate the following tips into your networking efforts:

1. **Talk to Strangers.**
   Will Rogers said, "A stranger is just a friend that I haven't yet met." Be open to networking anywhere and any place, including vacation, your children's after-school activities, while standing in line, and so on. If you are willing to strike up a conversation with a stranger, you may just experience the magic of networking. Likewise, at an event, do not be afraid to ask to join a conversation.

2. **Stand, Don't Sit.**
   When you sit down, you are confined to only talk to the people sitting in close proximity to you. In the same respect, don't hide behind tables, decorations, or groups of people. Be approachable by being visible. Stand and be mobile, ready to connect and engage with other people.

3. **Be Prepared.**
   Never leave home without your business cards. If you do not leave home without your driver's license, then why would you leave home without your business

cards? Get in the habit of presenting your card to others. Ask them: "Would you like to exchange business cards?"

4. **Build Rapport.**
Building rapport is always Job #1 in any networking situation. Listen twice as much as you talk. Find common ground. Mirror and match the other person. Make a human connection, starting with a professional firm handshake and appropriate eye contact.

5. **Quality, Not Quantity.**
Networking is a targeted strategy that can grow your business like a strong word-of-mouth campaign. You are better off making a few good connections than a dozen glancing blows at a networking event. Do not look around to see whom else you could be talking to. Focus on the person in front of you, your new friend. Make that person feel valued. Connect with that person.

6. **Discount No One.**
Everyone has value. Open yourself to receiving their gifts. A connection with a person, whether or not you are alike or as different as the seasons, could lead to many more opened doors. You never know whom they know who could help you.

7. **Follow Up.**
No matter how you choose to stay in touch with your contacts, you should be following up every five to six weeks with your top networking contacts, quarterly with mid-level contacts. Pick a systematic method that works for you and stick to it.

8. **Be Searchable.**
Unless you are in the witness protection program, make it easy for people to find you by registering for several social on-line networking sites such as LinkedIn.com, Plaxo.com, Facebook.com, and Twitter.com. Keep your profile updated and look for people from your "lost network"; that is, people you used to know but have since lost contact with. People are conditioned to search online for what they need. Make yourself searchable and findable and connect with professional people online.

9. **Aim Higher; Get Warmer.**
Decide whom you want to connect with and find a way to make it happen through the people you already know. Set your sights high and connect with people of influence. Avoid making a cold call by asking your network for a

"warm introduction" to the person you want to meet. And remember to always introduce yourself to the speaker when you attend a seminar. These people can turn into a potential contact for you and you for them. That is how I met networking extraordinaire Kathy McAfee.

10. Help Others, Ask for Help.

This is the spirit in which you should approach networking. Networking is about giving and receiving, exchanging information, and being resources for your networking community. You must be good at both sides of this equation. When someone asks you what you need or how he or she can help you, be ready to answer. Know what you need and whom you want to connect with before leaving any networking event, always ask, "Is there someone in your network that would make a good connection for me?" You will be amazed at how quickly your network grows!

As attorneys, our communication is often a one-way street. Whether through courtroom argument or position briefs, we tend to convey our message without seeking input or a reply from the listeners. We are striving for our words to be heard, to be believed, and to be accepted.

Networking is not about communicating to people but rather about communicating with people, which is often contrary to our professional practice. Learning to listen and connect with people is the way relationships are built and rain is made for your business. The next time you would rather go home and relax in front of the television set after a full day of work rather than attend yet another Chamber of Commerce event, think about all of the missed opportunities you are letting pass you by. Get motivated. Get connected. Get clients.

7

CONTROLLING CLIENT CONFLICT

"A conversation is a dialogue, not a monologue."
—*Truman Capote*

Fickle.
Unpredictable.
Unreasonable.
Uncooperative.

These words could easily describe several of your clients at any given time. However, these traits are not fatal to your rapport with your client. Building a mutually respectful and communicative relationship with clients depends on awareness—awareness of their personality types, of their emotions, and of their needs. How do you become aware? You watch and listen.

What does the client need from you? This does not mean what do they want, but rather how can you help them transcend the obstacles that are preventing them from reaching their legal goals and needs? Client awareness begins from the first consultation and should build and be re-evaluated throughout the relationship.

See Appendix B for intake, retainer, and many other forms that you will find useful in your practice.

THE INITIAL CONSULTATION

In an initial consultation, you should be engaging in three conscious steps: check for conflicts, screen the clients, and make an informed decision. When you fail to adequately complete any one of these steps, you are opening the doors to either a malpractice suit or a troubled attorney-client relationship.

Checking conflicts for the solo practitioner is a simpler process than it is for a 200-lawyer firm, but it still needs to be done carefully and diligently. Conduct a conflict check to determine whether a prospective client or a potential adverse party or witness has ever been a client of your office. As soon as a conflict surfaces, end the consultation and do not give legal advice nor ask any further questions of the client. This would be a good time to refer the client to another attorney. Make sure you let the other attorney know that you are sending a new client in his or her direction. Hopefully, one day the favor can be returned.

Screen potential clients carefully and thoroughly to weed out problem clients. Problem clients are easy to identify if you pay attention to their words and attitude towards the legal process. The following are typical of a problem client:

- ✔ The client wants everything done in a hurry.
- ✔ The client seeks reinforcement of their objectives and refuses all other available options
- ✔ The client states that they do not like attorneys.
- ✔ The client withholds information from you and asks why you need to know the requested information.
- ✔ The client has made suing a hobby or source of income.
- ✔ The client has hired and fired multiple attorneys on the same matter.
- ✔ The client has an outstanding bill due to another attorney.
- ✔ The client never admits his or her own fault but rather blames everyone else for his or her misfortune.
- ✔ The client is preoccupied with your fees.

At this stage, you have the information available to you to make an informed decision about whether you want your name associated with this client's legal problem. Consider the subject matter, the client's expectations, and your own gut instinct before you agree to accept a matter. It is best to avoid the problem clients before they become your problem; however, it is inevitable that you will be retained by a gem of a client to later learn she is only a pebble. Sometimes you cannot easily terminate the representation, so you need to make the best of a conflicted relationship.

THE FIVE CONFLICT MANAGEMENT STYLES

Conflict is inevitable in our line of work. Conflict not only arises between opposing parties, but is just as prevalent among clients and their counsel. Conflict that is not understood and managed effectively between the client and attorney can rupture your relationship with your client.

How a client handles conflict is indicative of what he or she needs from you as the advocate. There are five basic conflict management styles, one of which a client will likely adopt to resolve a stressful legal matter. If you identify and understand how the client copes with conflict, you can tailor your communication to fit the client's personality. As you read the following conflict management styles, you will probably be able to immediately associate each style to someone you know already:

1. **Competing**

   The client desires to win at the expense of the other party by dominating and bullying. He puffs up his shoulders and encroaches on the person's space whom he is trying to bully. He speaks loudly and threatens that he will either do some thing or not do something if the other person does not agree to his demands. If your client is the bully, you will need to place a strong hold on him in order to gain control of the relationship and have an impact on the case; otherwise, you become a puppet instead of counsel.

2. **Accommodating**

   The client tries to appease the other party through self-sacrifice in order to avoid disputes and maintain a relationship. This client will agree to anything so long as it keeps the peace. You need to build this client's confidence before you go to court or allow the client to make any decisions. This client needs you to assert their rights and be their voice; otherwise, they will agree to much less than they are entitled.

3. **Compromising**

   The client attempts to resolve a conflict by identifying a solution that is partially satisfactory to both parties, but not completely satisfactory to either. This is the model client who recognizes the benefit of compromise and will rationally and methodically analyze all available options to reach an outcome that is not wonderful, but is livable for everyone involved. These clients are rare.

4. **Collaborative**

   The client cooperates with the other party to understand their concerns and express their own concerns in an effort to find a mutually and completely satisfactory solution. Be wary of the collaborative client because although he is a gem in principal, he will be difficult to satisfy. Very rarely does litigation result in two satisfied customers. When there is the expectation for complete satisfaction for both, there will ultimately be disappointment when those expectations are not realized. Explain to this client that, although his efforts are admirable, his vision may be impossible.

5. Avoidance

The client is uncooperative and unassertive. She is indifferent to everything and wants the matter to resolve on its own. This client does not return phone calls nor listen to your advice. She believes that inaction is the best action. To handle this client, document everything in writing to the client. If the client continues to disassociate from the matter and your services, you should seek termination of representation. Be sure to advise the client of your intentions in writing and set a date in which they need to respond. If you still do not hear from the client, get out of the case. You can only help those who will help themselves.

Conflict between client and counsel is likely to arise at one time or another during the course of representation. Some researchers maintain that all conflict is built upon the parties' perception of incompatible goals. At first clients assume that you, as their attorney, want the same thing as them, no matter the cost. If you deviate from the client's objective, conflict builds and the client becomes aware of differences in goals and may see his or her attorney as an obstacle to goal attainment, rather than a means to reach their goals. The challenge and burden falls on the attorney to express, shape, and curb conflict so that common ground can be reached and the relationship between attorney and client is salvaged.

The best way to handle an unruly client is through confrontation and problem solving. Confront the problem in a gentle and tactful manner rather than become defensive or combative. The following is a methodical way to handle a conflicted relationship:

1. Acknowledge the problem (i.e., lack of communication, different goals, expectations).
2. Set a face-to-face meeting with your client to identify the problem.
3. Ask your client, "What do you expect from me?" Tell your client what you expect.
4. Come up with a solution that both of you agree on...and then proceed accordingly.
5. If a resolution cannot be reached, discuss whether you are the best advocate for your client going forward. Refer the client to someone else.

6. Document the meeting in written correspondence so there is no confusion about what transpired.

Sometimes clients cannot tell you what it is they expect of you. They just want you to spend all of your time trying to "win" the case. In a situation like this, you cannot keep your client happy because you are never doing enough.

Never react. If a client calls you enraged and starts saying things to you that are emotional and irrational, explain that you have a few things you need to get done but that you will call back in one hour so you will have time to discuss any concerns in more detail. Usually this gives the client time to cool off, and it prevents you from saying anything just as emotionally charged.

Remember that your values and sanity come first.

10 Tips to Keep Your Clients Happy

You want to be the first person a client calls no matter what type of legal problem he or she has. You can decide whether to take a matter yourself or refer it out, but you become the gatekeeper and the person the client is talking about when he or she says, "Let me talk to my lawyer first." When clients feel connected to you, you will bring in more business, more revenue, and more profits through either repeat business or referrals. Engage in the following 10 tips to pave the path to obtaining a lifetime client.

1. **Be accessible.**
   Adhere to the 24-hour rule—every client will get a return phone call or e-mail within 24 hours. Even if you do not have time to speak to the client, call (or have staff call) and inform the client that you cannot speak at that moment but that you did receive the message and you will call back later that day or tomorrow. Clients appreciate being acknowledged.

2. **Copy the client on all communication.**
   Correspondence, pleadings, court notices. No matter the insignificance or significance of a document, the client should receive a copy. Send clients status reports each month if it's appropriate for the type of cases you are handling. The client should be receiving more mail from you than just your monthly bill. Well-informed clients are less likely to complain, more likely to refer business, more likely to pay your bill, and less likely to grieve you.

3. **Understand the client's needs.**
   Forge relationships by knowing your client. Often clients believe a need is

unmet when something does not happen the way they would like it to happen. Try to understand the motivation behind their actions and words. Cope with angry clients by acknowledging their feelings and trying to address their concerns by spending time speaking to them, explaining the legal process, and discussing options and potential outcomes. By identifying and addressing your client's needs, the client will feel like he or she is understood, and the perception of you and the services you offer will swell.

4. **Do not underestimate the spoken word.**
   While e-mails are convenient, there is no better way to communicate with a client than to pick up the phone. Often dialogue diffuses tense situations—just by exchanging thoughts and ideas, the client may feel like his or her expectations are being met. A client who expects one and only one outcome will be satisfied with nothing less than that outcome. Take the time to discuss other potential scenarios. Other outcomes may be just as beneficial to a client, even if cloaked in different terms. You need to make your client aware of all options.

5. **Treat clients like people.**
   Clients like to do business with people they like. One way to enhance the likability factor is to show them you care. Make notes of family members' names and other personal information so that your conversation can transcend business. This tells your clients that you care about them and that you listen to them. For example, ask a client how his ill parent is doing or whether the college send-off of his son went well. On the other hand, if the client feels like you are always trying to get rid of them when you are on the phone, they will remember.

6. **Work as a team.**
   Clients need to feel that they are part of the process. The legal process is often a scary and unexplored territory for most of our clients. They feel powerless in these situations. Consult with them every step of the way so they feel like they have some control. This is also a malpractice-preventative measure. A client cannot point a finger at you for an adverse outcome if they were part of the decision-making process.

7. **Act and speak honestly.**
   Always tell the client the worst-case scenario and do not make empty promises. The result: they will appreciate your forthrightness, even if they do not like what you are saying. When you try to bend rules or use questionably unethical tactics to act on your client's behalf, you are undermining your reputation. Perception is everything, and if someone perceives you as dishonest, you will

have a difficult time shaking that image. When clients ask you to do something, they wanted it done yesterday. Do not promise a client that a motion will be filed and not get around to it for three weeks. Be truthful about time frames. They will lose faith in your word otherwise. Not only is acting ethically good for your relationships with your clients, it is also your obligation and duty as an attorney.

8. **Appear organized.**
A cluttered and full office does not mark a successful attorney, but rather it means you have lost control of your caseload, and clients may wonder if you will be able to give their case adequate attention. If a client starts to doubt your abilities as their advocate, the relationship will break down. Appearance is everything. You may be a brilliant trial attorney in the courtroom, but if it appears that you do not have control over the case, your office, or your time, your credibility starts to crumble.

9. **Ask questions.**
How did the receptionist treat you? Do you understand what we talked about? Is there anything else I can do for you? Do you need to hear from me more or less? What are your objectives? Were you satisfied with my representation of you? When you ask questions, not only does the client feel like they are part of the legal process, but you also get some insight into what is working and not working in your practice.

10. **Do not keep clients waiting.**
Your client's time is just as valuable as yours, so don't keep anyone waiting more than 15 minutes. If a client is waiting an hour for you to appear in court or in your reception area, the client's trust in you will erode. Keeping people waiting shows a lack of respect and implies inefficiency and disorganization.

Preventing Legal Malpractice

Solo and small firms tend to be the focus of disciplinary action. When a new associate at a large firm makes a mistake, the client typically complains to a senior level attorney and the problem is remedied; however, when a new solo attorney makes the same error, there is no one to complain to except the state bar association or disciplinary agency. For this reason, solo and small firm practitioners need to be even more cautious because a public disciplinary order tarnishes an attorney's reputation for years.

According to the American Bar Association (March, 1997), the top ten areas of law sued for malpractice include:

✔ personal injury: plaintiff
✔ real estate
✔ business transactions
✔ domestic relations
✔ corporate/business organization
✔ collection/bankruptcy
✔ estate, trust, and probate
✔ criminal
✔ workers' compensation
✔ personal injury: defense

A client's perception of your services is often tainted by strong emotions about their legal problems. You are expected to perform miracles at times and when you fail to do so, the client may criticize your skills. The reason for a claim varies—failure to timely file pleadings, improper advice or drafting of a document, failure to advise, unethical conduct, failure to provide a written fee agreement, and mishandling of funds are just a few common causes of action surrounding malpractice lawsuits.

Tips to Avoid Malpractice

As a practicing attorney, you are exposed to a potential lawsuit every day of your career; however, if you do the following, you will limit the likelihood of such an occurrence:

✔ Do not accept a case if it is outside your area of practice regardless if business is slow.
✔ Talk to your client frequently. Let your client know the status of the case, all available options and outcomes, expected and incurred fees and expenses, and make decisions about the case together.
✔ During the initial consultation, obtain enough information to determine if you are conflicted out of the case.
✔ Never guarantee or promise a certain result.
✔ Confirm everything in writing with both your client and opposing counsel—decisions, offers, demands, agreements, and so on.
✔ Use a docket or practice management system to ensure deadlines are not missed.
✔ Document every phone call that you make.
✔ Upon the completion of a matter, confirm the termination of services in written correspondence and include a financial accounting of the matter.

✔ Maintain meticulous accounting of your trust account. The shortest path to disbarment runs through the trust account.

✔ Properly screen and evaluate potential clients and cases. If you have an unexplained bad feeling about the matter, trust your instinct and turn the case away. If you turn down a case, send a non-representation letter and return all of the client's documents.

In the event that you are the recipient of a malpractice claim, you will be relieved that you purchased professional liability insurance coverage. While not every state requires professional liability insurance of practicing attorneys, it is foolish and risky to decline coverage to save on overhead expenses. Without insurance, defending against a claim could be the demise of your business. Countless billable hours will be lost defending the matter and the legal fees to hire defense counsel could put you out of business.

When you research various insurance options, you will come across the following terms:

✔ **Claims Made Coverage:** Coverage applies to claims made against the insured within the time period covered by the policy regardless of when the incident actually occurred. All liability insurance is "claims made"; however, many policies exclude prior acts coverage unless it is specifically stated in the policy.

✔ **Prior Acts or Retroactive Dates:** If the policy does not offer full prior acts coverage, the policy may specify a retroactive date that signals the earliest date for coverage.

✔ **Tail Coverage:** Provides an extended period of coverage after a firm dissolves or cancels its current policy or an attorney retires or leaves a practice to assume a position either teaching or on the bench.

Do not select an insurance company based purely on the lowest quote received. Instead, be sure the company is established and has a relationship with a local bar association. The companies that work in conjunction with a bar association typically offer the best rates and coverage and are most used by other attorneys in your jurisdiction. At a minimum, you should obtain $1 million in coverage. Questions to ask the insurance company include:

✔ Is there a deductible?

✔ Are defense costs outside the limits of liability your responsibility? When defense costs are inside the liability limits, every dollar spent defending a claim reduces the remaining limits of liability.

✔ Is anyone besides yourself covered under the policy?

✔ Are there conditions that must be complied with before coverage ensues?

Client conflict is inevitable in our profession, so be proactive about preventing malpractice. From the moment a client enters your office, you should be evaluating the case and client. If you decide to accept a case, you need to be nurturing the client relationship. When conflict arises, address it immediately and professionally. Be aware of how you handle conflict also.

Fickle.
Unpredictable.
Unreasonable.
Uncooperative.

Be sure that these same words used to describe a client are not used to describe you.

8

SETTING AND COLLECTING FEES

"A professional is someone who can do his best work when he doesn't feel like it."
—Alistair Cooke

You cannot go to a hair salon and tell the hairdresser that she should bill you at the end of the month for your haircut. You cannot eat in a restaurant and tell the waiter that you are going to enjoy your dinner, but you will be back in 30 days to pay the bill. Then why do we allow clients to reap the benefits of our services without first paying for the services? We may be allowing it to happen by virtue of our own conduct.

While several billing options should be considered as you establish your fees, the bottom line is this: It is your obligation and duty to set fees that correspond with the anticipated output needed to resolve the matter. Some practice areas do not require payment by billable hours, but chances are if you plan on having a general practice, somewhere along the way you will need to capture the time you spent on a file. Even if you are being paid on a contingency basis or flat fee, it is still a good idea to track the time spent on the file just in case you need to defend yourself or your fees in a grievance.

The way you capture and bill your time will not strengthen the attorney-client relationship, but it can certainly weaken it. The client who calls each month questioning your billing methods is the client who likewise will lose trust in your legal skills. You must set appropriate fees, create client-friendly invoices, and implement good billing procedures.

THE CONNECTION BETWEEN FEES AND SERVICE

A happy client is one who is more likely to pay the bill. Keeping a client happy has less to do with your actual legal skills and more to do with building a trusting and respectful relationship with your client. How we deliver services and how we communicate this deliverance is how we foster positive, productive business relationships with clients. If we send a client an invoice at the end of the month showing 4.5 hours of legal work performed, yet that was the one and only communication you had with the client all month, the client will raise an eyebrow. However, if throughout the month you copy the client on all correspondence, send quick e-mails to provide an update on the progress of the case, and speak to the client on the phone several times, when the client receives your invoice, he or she will feel like you have been working for the same cause and will be less likely to doubt your fees.

You need to make sure that your expectations are aligned with those of your clients. It is imperative that you discuss fees with your client from the outset. You do not want to underestimate legal fees any more than you want to overstate fees.

✔ Discuss the scope of the engagement. Exactly what does your representation include and not include? For example, does it include appeals? Does it include post-judgment action? What services will require additional fees?

✔ What are your rates and how are they calculated? Are your fees tied to results? Do you bill hourly? Do you offer a fixed fee?

✔ Discuss the retainer fee. How will the client know when it has been exhausted? How will the client know how it is being used? Will you require an additional retainer fee before the prior is exhausted? How much?

✔ How often will you send invoices out? What will be included on the invoice? Will interest be charged on late fees?

✔ Discuss legal costs. Who is responsible? Do you expect that they are paid before they are incurred or will you front the costs and expect reimbursement? What are the anticipated legal costs for a particular case?

✔ What is the anticipated length of engagement?

✔ Does your fee include unlimited communication or will the client be billed for phone contact or e-mail correspondence?

One size does not fit all. You have the option to calculate fees as traditionally or as creatively as you see fit. Below are different fee options to consider:

✔ **The hourly fee:** Be sure the fee is comparable to the going rate for your practice area and community. Discuss whether the client will be charged for phone calls with you. I do not like to charge for calls between myself and my client. I think this breaks down communication and the client always feels like there is a stopwatch at the other end of the phone.

✔ **The fixed fee:** Set a fee based on the information available to you at the beginning of the engagement that covers the entire cost of the engagement. You can also create an incremental fixed fee; that is, you quote the client a flat fee in stages. After the completion of each stage, you quote them how much the next stage will cost and what it will include. If you elect this method, it is important to discuss all the stages with each client and the anticipated costs prior to the engagement so that the client is not surprised down the road.

✔ **Contingency:** Based on results. Typically used in personal injury cases so that the more the client settles for or wins, the more you receive.

A DISCUSSION OF FIXED FEES

Imagine a world in which you receive your entire fee before doing any legal services—a world in which you do not need to chase clients for payment. Clients are as unique as their cases. The future of fee-setting is one in which the client and attorney reach a customized fixed fee arrangement that allows enough flexibility for "change orders" when clients express additional needs or when unforeseen circumstances arise.

By setting a flat fee for specified services, you avoid future disputes over fees, discussions about discounting your bills, and collection efforts. Clients who accept this arrangement will know what they are getting for their money and will have pre-paid for these services already.

Quoting fixed fees projects your confidence, experience, and assertiveness. If you charge by the hour, the client may often feel like you are prolonging a case in order to line your pockets. With a fixed fee, this thought will never enter your client's psyche because the fee is not about paying for your time by the minute. By quoting a fixed fee, you are telling the client that you have enough confidence and trust in your skills to offer value pricing. A client can be assured that you do not benefit from drawing out the length of the case. You are forced to work effectively and productively. Your objectives and goals are aligned with your client's objectives and goals.

Change orders are designed to cover work that falls outside the scope of your initial fee arrangement or when the unexpected occurs. Be sure to discuss this with the client and include it in the fee agreement. For example, fix a fee for divorce representation that covers all aspects of the litigation except for trial preparation and trial. The client should be aware at what point the fixed-fee arrangement ends and trial preparation begins so that additional fees are warranted. A new fee agreement should be signed at this point.

Offering fixed fees differentiates your firm from others who adhere to the more traditional hourly billing. An attorney who offers a more traditional approach cannot offer the client assurance about how much it will cost to litigate the case. The client goes into that relationship blindly. The attorney who offers a fixed-fee arrangement is reassuring the client that the legal fees will not exceed the fixed rate. The client enters into that attorney-client relationship with eyes wide open and knows what the attorney will be doing to fulfill the client's legal needs.

EFFECTIVE BILLING PRACTICES

Whether or not you are paid hourly, tracking your time as you perform the work is a smart practice. It is easier to do this as you go along rather than try to recreate it later. Even if you do not charge clients for specific activities, such as attorney-client phone calls, you should still track your time so clients can see all the work you have performed. If your clients see an hour of work for which they were not billed, they will feel like they received something for free. Everybody likes to feel like they got a bargain.

Furthermore, by documenting all of your time, you can see your real-time investment in a case. You will be better able to decide whether a discount is warranted or evaluate how much time is needed to handle a future matter that is similar in nature—helpful information to have if you offer fixed-fee pricing.

Your bills should be easy to understand. Do not code your work in initials and abbreviations so that the client cannot understand it. Each entry should include:

- ✔ What?
- ✔ Why?
- ✔ When?
- ✔ How Long?

Rather than write "Research," say "Researched relevant termination of parental rights case law to determine whether an appeal is appropriate."

Or rather than "Phone call with opposing counsel," say "Phone call with opposing counsel to discuss division of personal property."

You should track your time with an automated program. While you can capture your time manually by simply inserting a records time chart into each file, this method is not the most productive because at the end of each month you will need to re-create the chart in an invoice. Likewise, you need to track client expenses in a separate log that will need to be transferred to the monthly invoice. Regular client expenses can include:

- ✔ copying expense
- ✔ postage expense, including UPS or Federal Express

✔ facsimile expense
✔ court fees
✔ marshal service fees

If you do not track these expenses, you could be losing money for your company. Automated billing programs allow you to input your time as well as client expenses and generate invoices with a click of the mouse. The billing programs available are numerous. They vary in price and features. Some programs cater to large firms while others offer a more limited program, but one that may be sufficient for your start-up practice. Some programs offer calendaring, tickler systems, case management, and billing functions all in one. The following list is not exhaustive, but it offers a summary of different software programs available.

ABACUS LAW

Features: one of the most inclusive billing systems with credit card integration, employee productivity reports customized billing, 1099 reporting, one year of technical support, unlimited access to e-classes, data protection, general ledger, electronic billing.
Cost: price quotes are only good for seven days following a request, but you can plan on spending approximately $1,500 for the timekeeper and approximately $1,000 for each additional timekeeper.
Web site: www.abacuslaw.com
To purchase: call (800)726-3339.

BILL4TIME

Features: automated backups; Web-based, unlimited free technical support, free product upgrades, billing rate flexibility, restricted employee access, billing from hand-held devices.
Cost: $39.99 per month per user.
Web site: www.bill4time.com
To purchase: purchase online or speak to a representative at (877)245-5484.

RTG BILLS

Features: promotes easy-to-use system, computerized stopwatch, separate fees and expense entries, offers free support via e-mail, free upgrades for one year, RTG

Timer allows you to bill on your handheld device.

Cost: $95 with no additional cost for each timekeeper. RTG Timer is free for the first timekeeper and $15 for each additional timekeeper.

Web site: www.rtgsoftware.com

To purchase: purchase online and download program.

Tab3

Features: comprehensive billing software for either solo practitioners or large law firms; stopwatch timers track as you work; edit, reprint,or unbill at any time; billing rate flexibility; accounts receivable reports; employee productivity reports; security feature allows restricted access.

Cost: a single-user costs $295 for the software license. Optional annual maintenance is offered at an additional $105. Palm handheld software available for additional $75 for a single user.

Web site: www.Tabs3.com

To purchase: locate an authorized re-seller at (402)423-1440 or send an e-mail to info@Tabs3.com to purchase software.

Time59

Features: Web-based; accessible from handheld devices, automatic backup of data, time and expense tracking, invoicing, e-mail invoices to clients, accounts receivable reports, not specifically designed for attorney use only.

Cost: $49.95 per year for unlimited use; 30-day free trial.

Web site: www.time59.com

To purchase: purchase online or speak to a representative at (312)957-4711.

Tussman Program

Features: billing, general ledger, and calendar, can be purchased together or separately; billing program performs conflict checks; generates bills and management reports; distinguishes entries for billable hours and costs.

Cost: $595 for just the billing program. Additional $100 to add the calendar. Additional $200 to add the general ledger. Also additional cost for multi-user version of program

Web site: www.tussman.com

To purchase: purchase by calling (800)228-6589 to download program.

Before you commit to a billing program, look at sample pages on the program's Web site so you can determine how user-friendly it is. It is much more difficult to switch a billing program once you start using one so do not just select the most cost-effective program, but rather research, speak to the program representatives, compare, and then choose wisely based on your needs.

METHODS OF ACCEPTING PAYMENT

The more payment options you give a client to pay your bill, the more likely you will be paid. Although accepting personal checks may be risky, the convenience for clients may far outweigh the risk. If you were to tell your client that he or she needs to provide a money order or bank check, you risk the person walking out the door and not coming back. Accept the check and wait for it to clear before you begin performing work on the case. If a check is returned for non-sufficient funds, call the client immediately and ask when the check can be redeposited or if he or she can send you a bank check. Explain to the client that you need to charge a returned check fee and that you will not commence work on the case until payment is confirmed.

Accepting credit cards is the avant garde way to get paid. Although there is a fee to accept credit cards, it is minimal compared to the costs of an unpaid bill. As a merchant who can accept credit card payments, you can do so over the phone, in person, by e-mail, or mail.

I had a client who retained me from Texas. His wife filed for a divorce in Connecticut. He needed a lawyer in Connecticut and did not have time to shop around. We spoke on the phone and he paid the retainer by credit card. If I did not accept credit cards, I would have had to wait for him to send me a check that would have delayed the case by weeks or he could have decided to shop around before he retained an attorney once he hung up the phone.

There are numerous ways to become a merchant. Your bank may offer such a service. Likewise, an independent service organization can act as a middleman between you and the bank. The monthly and transactional fees fluctuate from one service to another so shop around for the best deal. Merchant accounts usually charge to lease or buy the equipment so you can physically swipe cards; however, you do not need the actual equipment to take credit cards. Better to process credit cards through your accounting program such as Quickbooks.

Check with your local bar associations before you decide on a service organization. Some bar associations work with companies that cater to law firms to set up accounts that do not violate any rules on co-mingling funds. It is best to have the legal fees deposited into your client trust account and transactional fees withdrawn from your operating account. Otherwise, you should deposit the money into your operating account and as soon as the funds are available, move it to your client trust funds. Do not deposit the funds into your client trust account because transactional and monthly fees will be withdrawn from this account and the client should not be charged for these fees.

How to Get Paid

Some clients don't pay because they can't pay, not because they don't want to pay. Some clients just won't pay. It is easier to collect payment from the "can't pay" people than it is from the "won't pay" people.

If you determine the cause for non-payment, you can find a solution. If a client genuinely does not have the funds to pay a bill, discuss whether a payment plan can be agreed upon. Perhaps the client can pay you from a tax refund. Although a lump sum payment is unlikely in situations like these, little payment over time is better than no payment at all. So long as a client is willing to make an effort to pay, I never charge interest or late fees. As soon as the client misses a payment, I send a letter or invoice emphasizing that any additional missed payments will result in interest or late fee charges.

The client who can pay but refuses to pay is also the client who will likely respond to a fee collection suit with a counterclaim for malpractice. Some clients refuse to pay as a statement of dissatisfaction with your services. The key is to finding why these people are not happy with your services. If you identify the problem, you can address the problem and try to salvage the relationship. Request a meeting with the client, not to discuss your unpaid bill, but rather in an attempt to repair the attorney-client relationship. Let the client speak and listen. Show him or her you are listening by maintaining eye contact and by not getting defensive.

Ask the client: What aspects of my representation are you unhappy with?

Are there things that you have control over such as lack of communication with the client or is it something you have no control of such as the length of litigation?

Then ask yourself: Are there things you can do to repair this relationship? Can you continue with the representation based on the client's expectations?

Only after you have identified the client's concerns and expressed ways in which they will be addressed, ask the client about the outstanding bill. Perhaps, eliminate the interest or late fees to reach a resolution.

You should send out bills monthly or as soon as an engagement has ended. If a case wraps up on December 2 but you typically do not bill until the end of the month, generate a bill as soon as the engagement is over. The client's satisfaction will be fresh and they will probably be quicker to pay it while they are still grateful for your services.

Give client discounts. Send an invoice with the full fee and then show a courtesy discount.

Everyone likes to feel like they got a deal, so even if the discount is for a nominal amount, they still feel like they are getting a bargain.

If a client has not paid the bill, do not be afraid to call. It is easy to slip a bill into a junk drawer, but it is harder to say on the phone that he or she is ignoring your bill. Keep the conversation friendly, yet assertive, but do not attack the person. Tell them you noticed that the bill is overdue and you wanted to remind them. Ask the client if they need another bill sent. Tell the client you can accept payment by credit card and ask when you can expect payment. The message you want to send is that you manage your financial matters with the same assertiveness and diligence as you do your cases. If you are unassertive about collecting fees, the clients will take advantage of that. Sometimes a letter indicating that you will be terminating representation is enough to get the client to write you a check. Lastly, if it looks like you will not be paid, then it may be time to actually terminate representation.

DON'T TAKE THE DUDS

A deadbeat client is one who wants "something for nothing." How do you weed out the duds?

While you can sometimes identify a problem client during just a phone call, more often you will need the initial consultation to identify the problem clients. The following is a list of client behavior observed at the initial consultation that typically signifies future fee collection headaches:

- ✔ Be wary when one of the first questions a client asks is: "How much do you charge?" Although at some point every client is going to ask this question, the client that raises this question before he removes his coat is the client who will likely always question your bills and rarely pay them.
- ✔ If a client has changed attorneys more than once, you can be assured that he or she has set unreasonable expectations of the attorney. If you agree to accept the case, you too will soon find yourself on the list of attorneys who did that client wrong, especially if the last attorney's bill remains unsatisfied.
- ✔ When a client responds to your fee quote by saying, "The attorney I met with yesterday only quoted me a $1,500 retainer," you should respond, "Then perhaps you should retain that attorney because I cannot discount my services that much."
- ✔ Be careful of the client who has represented himself for the past several months but now wants you to appear in court tomorrow at his contempt hearing.
- ✔ Any client who gets agitated when you ask for the retainer before you file an appearance in the case has no intention of paying your full fee.
- ✔ Stay clear of a client who refuses to acknowledge wrongdoing in a situation but instead makes excuses for bad conduct and blames everyone else for problems.
- ✔ Watch out for the client who shows up with a shopping bag filled with

documents. I had a deadbeat client who dropped off additional documents every week; they were always unorganized, always coffee-stained, and always incomplete. To date, her bill remains unpaid.

✔ When a client insists on legal advice before scheduling an appointment for a consultation, he or she is most likely just looking for free advice.

When you identify a potential problem client, either secure a hefty retainer up front or send the client on her way. Go with your gut. If it smells bad, it probably is bad.

9

Winning the War on Chaos: Time and Paper Management

"Make everything as simple as possible, but not more so."
—*Albert Einstein*

Organization is the ability to take command of the daily chaos of your solo practice. For whatever reason, we tend to think that if our office is stacked with files that overflow onto the guest chair and floor, then we are busy and successful attorneys. However, an office that is swimming in stacked files, unopened mail, unreviewed faxes, and unread publications, is also the office of missed opportunities, lost information, and incomplete task lists.

"Begin each day with the end in mind," teaches author and professional speaker, Dr. Stephen R. Covey in *The Seven Habits of Highly Effective People* (Free Press, 1989). Each day you should identify clearly defined goals. Your goals should be specific and achievable. Do not set a goal to scan all case files onto your computer when you know you will be in court for most of the day. You are only setting yourself up for failure. In order to attain your goals, you need to be realistic about them.

Managing Your Day

Differentiate tasks from priorities. Priorities are actions that need to be taken in order to fulfill your goals. Tasks can easily distract you away from priorities. Although tasks need to be completed sometimes to meet your greater goal, the challenge is to keep your eye on the priorities and not allow tasks to lead you astray.

Start by thinking big and work down. Long- and short-term planning is essential to managing your time. You need to first write an ongoing master "to do" list. From that list you need to develop a daily "to do" list.

Look at the big picture first. Make a list of everything that needs to be done. Now ask yourself: What items on this list are priorities that need to be addressed immediately?

Separate your list into A, B, and C priorities. "A" items are important to your long-term success. "B" may be urgent but not as important. "C" are those that would be nice to do if you have the time.

Assign each task to a day of the week. Be as specific as possible. For example, rather than write "prepare for trial," write "compile exhibit list for trial." The more specific the assignment, the more manageable it is and the easier it will be for you to designate adequate time to complete it.

Break out large projects into smaller assignments to help stave off the feeling of being overwhelmed. Always start with the high-priority items. When you start with non-priority tasks because it is easier, you are procrastinating—a dangerous practice. Check off items as you complete them to give yourself a sense of accomplishment.

Once you create your "to do" lists, stay on track by doing the following:

- ✔ Update your lists frequently and regularly.
- ✔ Try to do your planning at the same time every day so that it becomes habit.
- ✔ Keep one planner with both your business and personal appointments—it is easier to manage your time when you are looking at one integrated calendar.
- ✔ Close your door and tell your receptionist to not disturb you for an hour or let voicemail pick up your phones, so that you can accomplish high-priority tasks.
- ✔ Schedule "busy work" into your day, such as opening mail or paying the bills— it doesn't need to be the same time every day, but it should be for the same amount of time.
- ✔ Do not over-schedule yourself—leave some downtime each day for things that may come up unexpectedly.
- ✔ Just do it—schedule your appointments immediately while you are on the phone.
- ✔ Schedule your personal life into your calendar; otherwise, you might find yourself saying that you are too busy to do the things you enjoy whether it's family, fitness, or recreation.
- ✔ Schedule your most demanding assignments for when your energy level is the highest.

SET UP A PRACTICE MANAGEMENT SYSTEM

Files that are not periodically reviewed are those that entice missed deadlines, late discovery, and little client correspondence. A practice management system is generally a database that collects and organizes information about a particular case and reproduces a physical file on the computer. One of the most impressive features of such a system is the access attorneys can have to files on their PDA or BlackBerry® device. WORLDOX® is a company that offers document management appropriate for solo and small firms because it does not require a separate server. WORLDOX organizes and indexes e-mail communications, scanned paper documents, word processing documents, spreadsheets, and anything else that can be stored as a file.

A practice management system is also a tool to check for client conflicts before you commence work on a file. It is impossible to remember names of every person you ever represented. A practice management system will allow you to check for conflicts by simply inputing a potential client's name into the system. A system will typically search for different spellings of the same name to prevent human error; however, in order to be assured your conflict check is accurate, you must be diligent about entering the identity of every person involved in a past or current matter, including consultations.

REMINDER SYSTEMS

You need to establish a method to make sure no deadlines or files slip through the cracks. Many malpractice claims are filed against lawyers as a direct result of failing to meet jurisdictional deadlines. For each file, you should calendar a diary date so that the file is looked at no less than every two weeks. Assign two to three files per day. Enter the file name on your calendar, preferably both paper and computerized. During your designated "quiet time" each day, look through the file and see what needs to be done and when. Make sure these dates are put on your calendar. My old employer used a simple system that worked for his practice for 30 years. Each file was given a diary date two weeks in the future. The file's date was entered into a log book. Each day the secretary would open the log book and pull the files entered for that day. Before the attorney re-filed a file, he would enter a new diary day that would then be entered into the log book. It is less about what type of system you use and more about using a system that works for you.

SETTING UP FILES

When a client is on hold on the telephone waiting for you to find his or her file, you want to be sure you can easily locate the file and the documents within the file without the assistance of a rescue dog. You can set up your filing system in one of the following ways:

✔ **Alphabetical order:** File according to the client's last name. Be sure to also include a reference on the file such as "Bankruptcy" or "Custody." This is the simplest system for a solo practitioner to implement.

✔ **Numerical:** Assign a file number for each client. This system provides an extra level of privacy because the client's name does not appear on the file; however, it also makes file retrieval more difficult as you will need to consult the master list to find the file you are looking for.

Variations of numerical filing include:

✔ Sequential numbering (ex. 100, 101, 102)
✔ Calendar numbering (ex. 2008-100, 2009-101, 2009-102)
✔ Code or initial prefix numbering (example, FA-100 for "family matters" and PI-100 for "personal injury matters")

An organized file makes for an organized attorney. Setting up files is not rocket science. Simply purchase two-sided files with fasteners. One side should be used for the intake sheet, retainer agreement, memos, notes, and all correspondence. The other side should consist of legal documents, such as pleadings, court notices, final copies of contracts, wills, real estate documents, and so on. If a file requires discovery, expert reports, appraisals, and other miscellaneous documents, these should be placed in a sub-file within the main file. The key is consistency. Every file should be set up the same so that you can easily and quickly find what you are looking for.

Remember to create and regularly update a master active file case list. Each week you should review the master list to remind yourself of what files need work or have been stagnant.

GUIDELINES FOR OPENING, CLOSING, AND DESTROYING FILES

Open a file when a client comes in for a consultation or anytime attorney-client privilege is created.

Close a file when there is nothing more to do in the matter. That means all outstanding bills have been paid or you have written off as bad debt. If there is potential future work to be done on a file, you should keep the file in your active file system.

Destroy a file as soon as you can. Notify the client that the file is being destroyed and that they may retrieve it prior to destruction. Do not destroy the file until you are sure that there are not any important documents in there that should be returned to the client, such as birth certificates, deeds, photographs, or any other document the client may want to retrieve. Keep in mind that a file is not limited to a paper copy but consists of all electronic data and communication also. Because file retention and destruction is state-specific, check the local rules in your jurisdiction before you begin tossing files.

In addition to your case files, you need to create office management files. You want to be able to find anything at a moment's notice. The only way to accomplish this lofty goal is to create a place for everything.

Create different file folders for office management files, such as:

- ✔ continuing legal education seminars and credits earned
- ✔ miscellaneous non-client related correspondence
- ✔ insurance information
- ✔ state business filing documents
- ✔ Web page and hosting information
- ✔ IRS and state tax documents
- ✔ supplier file for information on products and services
- ✔ invoice file

Make sure each piece of paper that crosses your desk relating to one of the above files gets filed away in the appropriate folder.

MANAGING THE PAPER CHAOS

As a new solo, chances are you will not be fortunate enough to pass the mundane task of sorting your mail to your secretary because you are the secretary. How often did you read and re-read the fax that came through the day before? The key to organizing all the paper that crosses your desk is to make a decision about what will happen with the document the first time you handle it. Carve out a half hour to forty-five minutes every day to review the mail. Immediately go through and discard all advertising, notices of seminars you will not attend, and other "junk mail." Stack magazines, journals, and other periodicals on a windowsill or other location that is not on your desk. Designate a location for all unpaid bills. All bills will go into this folder and will be reviewed at the end of each week or biweekly for payment. Now go through all correspondence related to an active file. Read the letter and immediately determine whether a response is necessary. If it is not, file the letter. If a response is necessary, jot down notes on what needs to be done to address the correspondence or pleading. Determine whether the correspondence needs to be addressed immediately or can be done within a certain time period.

Whenever possible, handle everything that can be done quickly as soon you can. If correspondence only requires a quick fax or phone call, do it so you can file the document away and forget about it. If you receive a notice of an upcoming court date, deposition, or other scheduled event, be sure to immediately place it on your calendar and make a notation if the client needs to be notified and if so, do it. By immediately taking care of the minor task, you avoid needing to look at the notice at a later date for purposes of client notification or forgetting that the client was never notified. All other documents that require more than just a quick response should be filed in one task folder. Be sure to designate a time frame in which it should be addressed. By going through this process, you no longer have paper being shuffled around on your desk to be read and re-read 10 times before you decide to act on it. Each morning you should go through the folder that contains these documents and respond accordingly. For documents that might require a lengthier response than just a reply letter, you should create a due date, anticipate how long it will take to research case law and draft the document, then add the assignment to your "to do" list. Block out small periods of time a week or two before it is due to work on it. This will allow you to take that important phone call while you are researching and not feel pressured due to time constraints.

At the end of every day, you should not have any loose papers floating around your desk. All correspondence and documents that crossed your path that day should either be filed away or in an appropriate folder. If you go through this process every day, the surface of your desk should remain under control and organized.

At any given time, I have between four and five unread professional magazines, journals, and newspapers waiting for the day when I have an hour or so to catch up on reading. Typically, they make the commute with me home and back again to the office, never being opened. Eventually, in a month or two when the current mailings are received, I forget that I never read the ones from a few months ago and they end up discarded in the trash. Few people have the time to read each publication cover to cover, but by not opening them at all, they could be missing out on valuable information that is relevant to their practice. Once a month, take a half hour and flip through all publications. Tear out the articles that you would like to read and place them in a folder and then discard the publication. It is easier to transport your "articles folder" home with you than all of the publications. Furthermore, you are more likely to read one article at a time while having your morning coffee or while eating lunch at your desk, than you are the entire publication.

MANAGING THE PAPERLESS CHAOS

Technology is a valuable tool if it is used properly. While e-mail can be a constructive tool to communicate with both clients and other attorneys, our inboxes also drown in personal e-mails, spams, forwards, and blast advertising. E-mail can lead you astray from your "to do" list. You will control your e-mail traffic rather than allow it to control you, if you follow some simple guidelines:

✔ Block off times to process your e-mail—two to three times per day should be enough and avoid the temptation to check your e-mail more frequently.

✔ Create separate e-mail folders for each case file as well as general office management—as soon as an e-mail comes in pertaining to a certain file, reply, if necessary, and then move it to the corresponding folder so that it does not sit in your inbox or sent mail box.

✔ Write descriptive subject lines so that you can easily find a topic-specific e-mail if you need to access it later on.

✔ Keep a contact list on your computer, so you can easily access client information.

✔ Delete all unnecessary mail—old messages congest your inbox, so delete old, duplicate, or reply-version copies and free up space for new incoming mail.

✔ If you are on a mailing list for which you have no interest, unsubscribe to the list.

Our lives are busy and all too often we respond to e-mails as soon as we receive them. We may be waiting to pick our child up from school or standing in line at the food store when we respond, quickly and often thoughtlessly. The following are a few e-mail etiquette tips as you embrace technology and enjoy the benefits of a mobile office:

✔ Carefully consider what you write. It is a permanent record and can easily be forwarded to others.

✔ When you reply to a message, be careful that you reply to just the person you want and not to a list of people because you inadvertently hit "reply all."

✔ DON'T TYPE IN ALL CAPS. This is perceived as shouting.

✔ Be careful with punctuation. If you use a lot of exclamation marks, it may come across as being angry even if that is not what you intended.

✔ Do not use acronyms in professional e-mails, such as BTW (by the way) or FWIW (for what it's worth).

✔ Check your spelling before sending an e-mail. It is easy to quickly reply to an e-mail and forget to proofread. Even though it's e-mail, it is still a reflection of your practice.

✔ Do not copy, cut, and paste documents into the e-mail. Special formatting may distort in the correspondence. Send the original document as an attachment.

STORING COMPUTER FILES

Most attorneys are not entirely comfortable with operating from a strictly paperless office. Instead, files consist of a combination of both paperless and electronic format. Computer files can be organized simply by creating a folder for each client and storing documents accordingly.

For the more technologically forward attorney, every paper document that comes into the office can be scanned and filed electronically. Implementing a paperless office requires some time and effort to scan documents on a daily basis but once it is done, the convenience of having every file at you fingertips is worth the effort. Operating from a paperless office is also a personal choice. Some people, like myself, like to look through a physical file rather than have to peruse a computer for the last pleading or correspondence that was received.

No matter how you decide to maintain files, security and privacy should be a priority. The following are a few tips to ensure files are secure and client confidentiality is maintained:

✔ Do not store files where clients can easily access them.
✔ If you share an office with other attorneys, be sure your files are secured in locked filing cabinets.
✔ Use passwords and log on usernames for all computers within your office.
✔ Do not just throw confidential documents in the trash. Shred documents first before discarding them.
✔ Store files in locked space so that others cannot easily access them.

PUTTING OFF PROCRASTINATION

Procrastination is a villain in our time management war. We do not procrastinate what is enjoyable; we procrastinate the dreaded. Those who fall prey to procrastination do so out of habit. Typically when we procrastinate, there is no justification, but rather it is an irrational postponement to the inevitable.

The following are eight tips to pummel procrastination:

1. Schedule your most unpleasant tasks for early in the day when your energy is the highest.
2. Break large assignments into smaller, more manageable tasks.
3. Do not let indecision drive procrastination. Address what decisions need to be made. Make them and move forward.
4. Develop a mental picture of what the completed project looks like. Focus on the end result, not just the process.
5. Allow yourself intermittent breaks as you work through a project, so you can re-charge and re-energize.
6. Set deadlines for different phases of the project and incorporate these deadlines into your daily "to do" lists.
7. Acknowledge that perfectionism is unachievable. Maintain your high standards,

but allow yourself to move onto another piece of the project even if it is not perfect.

8. Block off adequate, undistracted time to complete an unpleasant task. Close your door, turn your cell phone off, leave a message in your voicemail that you are unavailable for the afternoon.

Once you become comfortable with strategically and methodically managing your time, it will become second nature. The key is finding a method and system that works for you and sticking with it.

10

TO STAFF OR NOT TO STAFF

"Leadership is the art of getting someone else to do something you want done because he wants to do it."
—*Dwight D. Eisenhower*

A solo practitioner makes quick costume changes on any given day. Lawyer. Marketing Director. Chief Financial Officer. Human Resource Director. Boss. In the latter two roles, you must hire competent people and then provide leadership that encourages them to give their best efforts and loyalty. It's no wonder many sole practitioners insist on doing everything themselves. Hiring and managing employees is a daunting task. Business pressures place strains on human relationships, so the exercise of first staffing your office and then retaining good employees is not an easy one. However, it is a necessary one when your workload dictates the need for support staff beyond your singular self.

Your business' survival depends on hiring the right people. Failure to do so could have disastrous consequences.

✔ How do you find a competent employee?
✔ What questions do you ask a potential employee?
✔ What steps need to be taken once you hire an employee?
✔ How do you retain an employee once you have found someone who is skilled and trustworthy? What happens when you need to terminate the relationship?

This chapter is not just about staffing your office, but rather about staffing your office smartly.

EMPLOYEE OR INDEPENDENT CONTRACTOR?

As a one-man or one-woman show, you are only responsible for yourself. If you have a slow month, you do not need to fret about paying an employee. Overhead is lower because you do not need to offer any benefits. If you are fortunate enough, there will come a time when there is not enough of you to go around and you will need help.

To decide whether it is time to bring on an employee, evaluate what work you actually have for somebody else. Take two weeks of your daily task list and highlight which tasks you could have delegated to somebody else. Figure out how much time was spent on each task. Now think about what other tasks you would have an employee complete, such as clerical tasks, document preparation and calendaring, and dictation. Would this be enough work for a full-time employee or a part-time employee? It is important that when you hire an employee, he or she has continuous and challenging work with which to be occupied. Your business does not profit from an employee who spends hours playing solitaire on the computer waiting for you to filter work his or her way.

What would you be free to accomplish if you had an employee who lightens your workload? You are probably hiring an employee for the wrong reasons if your free time is spent on the golf course. However, if you now have more free time to schedule new client appointments, attend networking functions, or volunteer for speaking engagements, then you would benefit from the additional support.

If you share office space you can also share a secretary, meaning you share the expense of payroll and payroll taxes. This situation could get confusing so to make this person's job easier you should set up mailboxes with each attorney's name. Put the assignment in the box with a date when you would like it completed and how long it should take. The risk of this situation is that one attorney may pilfer all of the individual's time.

Perhaps the work that you would delegate ebbs and flows, so you do not need someone every day. Outsourcing work to an independent contractor may be a viable solution. Find a reliable professional who offers services at a per diem rate. For example, I used a bright, young woman who is also an attorney, but didn't want to work full-time following her son's birth. I fed her as much or as little work as I needed done. I sought her assistance in a wide variety of assignments, such as researching for this book, to drafting legal briefs, preparing complaints, and drafting wills.

Rates for outsourced work typically range from $25 to $50 an hour. The benefits of outsourcing work are numerous: you only pay for the work that is done, you do not pay payroll taxes, and you do not need to provide benefits. On the other hand, the individual is not there for clerical and office management tasks or a last minute project that needs to be completed by the end of the day.

Whether an individual is classified as an employee or an independent contractor will affect how you pay Federal Income Tax Withholding, Social Security (FICA) tax, and Medicare taxes. You do not deduct taxes when you pay an independent contractor, but rather you will send the independent contractor a 1099 at the end of the year if you paid over $600 to the individual in one year and the person is not incorporated.

DEFINING AN EMPLOYEE'S ROLE

If you do decide to hire support staff, it is important to define this individual's role. This will eliminate any confusion as to what your expectations are of him or her and equally what he or she can do to meet your needs. Compile a list of what you would like your employee to do. It is important when you define a job description, you distinguish between what skills an applicant must have versus those skills that you would prefer that they have.

The following is an example list of what an employer might expect from a person who fills a secretarial position:

- ✔ open and sort mail
- ✔ collect files pertaining to correspondence and pleadings received in the mail
- ✔ transcribe dictation within 1 to 2 days turnaround time
- ✔ bring the attorney's attention to files requiring action
- ✔ draft correspondence regarding discovery issues and meet with clients to review discovery responses
- ✔ answer phones
- ✔ return some calls on the attorney's behalf
- ✔ schedule appointments
- ✔ pull files before appointments, depositions, and court dates
- ✔ update the calendar
- ✔ maintain the file management system
- ✔ keep track of office supplies

By providing the employee a list of what the new job entails, you will reduce the chance of tasks being overlooked, because the employee was unaware of your expectations.

How to Find Competent Employees

Conduct a search for an employee by advertising in newspapers or trade magazines or following-up on referrals from business contacts and clients. When a person contacts you, you should conduct a preliminary phone interview to make sure the person has the basic qualifications to meet your objectives. Once you decide to invite someone in for an interview, have the applicant fill out an application form. This will provide you with minimal information, such as former employers, education, training, and certifications.

See Appendix B for an employee application form.

Give the applicant a brief description of your practice and then start asking open-ended questions. Ask the person about previous jobs. What did these jobs entail? Why is she looking to leave her present position? What did she find most satisfying about the former work she had done? What was least satisfying about her former work?

Before you end an interview, ask for references. Although the applicant may not want you to contact their current employer, you should be able to contact at least one former employer. Do not make a final decision until you have interviewed a few individuals and contacted their references. You do not want to leave people lingering so as soon as you realize that an applicant does not have enough experience or possess the necessary skills to fit your needs, tell them and continue your search.

Compensating Employees

Salary or wage will vary greatly depending on the location where you practice, the going rate, and experience level of the individual. Ask around what other small firm business owners are paying entry-level staff and offer a comparable salary. You will not be able to compete with what large firms are paying staff, so you need to offer additional fringe benefits to attract and keep good personnel.

Fringe benefits describe benefits other than wage or salary income. Typical benefits may include life insurance, health insurance, retirement benefits, or even benefits such as gym memberships or daycare subsidies.

Medical benefits are expensive, but for some, the deal breaker on whether or not they accept a job. Likewise, retirement plans can be expensive to administer and run. Shop around for plans for small businesses and meet with a financial advisor about setting up a 401(k) or other firm retirement plan. Look into your local bar association for plans. They usually offer plans at discounted rates that can be tailored to the small firm practice.

Establish a vacation pay policy. Many employers offer two weeks vacation after a year's service and three weeks or more after an additional period of time. Paid holidays are generally granted for the following days:

- ✔ New Year's Day
- ✔ Memorial Day
- ✔ 4th of July
- ✔ Labor Day
- ✔ Thanksgiving Day
- ✔ Christmas

Additional holidays which you may or may not decide to observe are:

- ✔ Washington's Birthday
- ✔ Lincoln's Birthday
- ✔ Presidents' Day
- ✔ Columbus Day
- ✔ Martin Luther King's Birthday
- ✔ Day after Thanksgiving
- ✔ National Election Day

Keep in mind that if your employee's religious practice differs from yours, there may be additional holidays that you are unaware of but which he or she may want to take off. Be respectful of his or her observance of religious holidays and never deny that time off.

Decide how many sick days an employee will be entitled to a year and what your policy will be on maternity/paternity leave. The Family and Medical Leave Act of 1993 requires private-sector employers with 50 or more employers to provide up to 12 weeks of unpaid, job-protected leave to care for a newborn or adopted child, care for a spouse or child with a serious medical condition, or due to the inability to perform a job because of the employee's own serious health condition. In addition, employers must maintain health insurance coverage during the period of leave. As a small firm, although not required to, you should offer the same job protection to your employees. Keep in mind, just because you are preserving their job for them, you are not obligated to pay them during this time off.

Establish a liberal policy for an employee who must take time off to care for a sick child. Allow the employee to use his of her own sick time for this purpose and not have to use vacation time for this purpose.

Once you decide to hire an employee, you should have the employee start during a week in which you are accessible to help her get situated, train her in office procedure, and meet with her about your expectations. Do not schedule your employee's start date the day before you have a trial when you know you will be frantic and stressed, or the day you start your vacation. On your employee's first day, take her to lunch or bring lunch in so you can begin to get to know her, not just as an employee, but as a person.

Have patience. You cannot expect someone to come into the office on the first day and do everything exactly as you like it. You need to show her how you like things done. However, do not micromanage either. People have different ways of doing things and just because it is not "your way," does not mean it will not work. You may find "their way" is more efficient and productive, so be open to change.

Once your employee is comfortable with the basics of the job, let her perform the job alone. Encourage her efforts and avoid looking over your employee's shoulders. If a mistake is made, point it out and explain what or how it can be fixed. Remember, your attitude sets the tone of the work environment. If your employee senses irritability, impatience, and frustration from you at the outset, she will adopt a manner and work ethic of the same kind. If you smile, encourage, and appreciate your employee, she will produce better work product and become loyal to you and your business.

HOW TO DELEGATE

"I can do it better myself."
"I can't trust anyone to do a good job."
"I don't have the time to show somebody how to do something."
"I'm the only person who knows how to do it."

People use all kinds of excuses to hold onto work that could otherwise be delegated. If you made the decision to hire a staff member, then delegate work to that person. Delegating is not a means to increase productivity but actually a way to multiply it.

Here are some tips to help you delegate:
- ✔ Give thorough and complete instructions.
- ✔ Delegate the objective, not the procedure.
- ✔ Outline the desired results, not the methodology.
- ✔ Set interim deadlines to see how things are going.
- ✔ Delegate to the right person .
- ✔ Spread delegation around and give people new experiences as part of their training.
- ✔ Be sure to delegate the authority along with the responsibility.
- ✔ Don't make people come back to you for too many minor approvals.
- ✔ Trust your employee to do well and don't look over his or her shoulder.
- ✔ Be prepared to trade short-term errors for long-term results.
- ✔ Give praise and feedback at the end of the project.

The Motivation Factor

People work for money. This is not a revelation. However, surprisingly, surveys and studies of employees rank financial compensation low on a job satisfaction scale. Rather, job security, advancement, employer appreciation, and task enjoyment are more important to employees. A happy employee is a loyal employee.

- ✔ Do not use your employees to run your personal errands.
- ✔ Do not give your employees an assignment at 4:45 p.m. that must be done by 5:00 p.m.
- ✔ Do not take out your bad day on your employees.
- ✔ Do not disrespect your employees.

These are the people who will catch your mistakes, point out an impending deadline, and who will listen to an angry client rant if you are not in the office.

Attorneys often forget that an employee is not opposing counsel in a contentious case or a hostile witness. Employees are fallible human beings, much like yourself. Using fear or condescending language towards employees serves only one purpose: to chip away at job satisfaction and ultimately, loyalty to you.

It is easy to get agitated about mistakes and take it out on an employee. However, as you retreat back to your office after such an occurrence, in your wake you leave an employee who is hurt, angry, and stressed. If the quality of an employee's work needs to be addressed, do so in the privacy of your office, not in front of clients or other employees. If there are interpersonal problems among staff, address the problem as soon as you realize it exists. Keep the communication between yourself and your employees open and clear.

Show your employees that you value their skills through outward conduct. Do little things that show them you appreciate their hard work. Have lunch brought into the office occasionally. Close the office early one summer day and host a family picnic or baseball outing. Give year-end bonuses, if you can afford to. Celebrate birthdays. Say thank you. Say you are sorry. You will be amazed at how much more productivity and quality work you receive from an employee who feels valued and appreciated rather than one who feels overworked and undervalued.

For the small firm, finding and retaining good employees is difficult when there are large firms that can offer a larger salary and more benefits. You need to foster loyalty by creating a work environment where fair rules and treatment are balanced with flexibility when it is needed to support the employee's personal and family life. This is the only way to retain happy and loyal employees.

OFFICE POLICIES

The small firm practitioner who does not develop an office policy manual has a fool for a human resources director. Most small offices do not create an office policy manual because they simply think they do not need one. A manual should be used as a guideline, but never as an employment contract. The purpose of an office manual is to ensure consistency in office policy and management.

What to include in an office policy manual:

✔ Introduction: Welcome, Organization of the Firm, Mission Statement
✔ Employment Policies: Equal Employment Opportunities, Sexual Harassment and Complaint Procedures, Privacy Rights, Personnel Records, Emergency and Safety Procedures
✔ Compensation Policy: Work Hours, Part-Time Employees, Overtime Policy
✔ Time-Off: Vacations, Holidays, Sick Leave, Jury Duty, Religious Observances, Paid-leave Policy
✔ Employee Reviews: Performance Reviews, Raise Policy (at the same time for everyone or at the anniversary of the employee's hire date?)
✔ Benefits: Health Insurance, Disability Insurance, Workers' Compensation, Dental Insurance, Retirement Plans
✔ Employee Conduct: Absenteeism and Tardiness, Drug-Free Work Environment, Discipline/Termination Policies, Internet and e-mail usage restrictions
✔ General Disclaimer: Example: This is not intended to be an all-inclusive list of office policies and procedures of this firm. It is a guide to help answer common questions and set forth guidelines under which this firm operates. This firm reserves the right to revise and change the policy manual at any time. Employment with this firm is "at will," which means that either you or the employer may terminate the employment relationship at any time. This manual does not constitute an employee contract.
✔ Acknowledgement Page: Example: I, the undersigned employee, have read and understand the policies set forth in the office manual. I understand it is only a general guide and that it may be revised or changed at any time. I understand that my signature below does not create an employment contract and that I am an employee "at will."

_____   _____
Employee Signature   Employer Signature

Conduct quarterly- or half-year reviews of staff.

This helps both you and your employees communicate about what is expected as well as what suggestions they may have to run a more efficient office. If you ask an employee "What suggestions do you have to improve the functioning of this office?" the employee will feel like he or she has a voice that is actually being heard.

Be a team by acting like a team. Schedule weekly or bi-weekly office meetings to discuss the upcoming weeks, schedules, and tasks that need attention. Even small companies need the regularity of formal meetings, so that everyone is operating as a cohesive unit.

When to Say Good-bye

Not every employee/employer relationship is a match made in heaven. If it has come time to terminate an employee's services with your firm, you must do so with dignity and with formality. Firing someone is an unpleasant task for the person doing it as much as it is for the person at the receiving end of the news. Schedule a meeting with your employee at the end of your day when you can be free from interruptions. Tell your employee the exact reasons why he or she is being terminated. Tell the employee what type of severance pay you will be offering. For a small firm, one to two weeks of salary is typical. Explain how the ex-employee can apply for unemployment compensation. If the person has skills that you can honestly recommend, offer to be a reference.

Do not talk about the terminated employee negatively to your other employees or attempt to paint the situation in a comical light. Any lack of tact or feeling you might show when terminating an employee will cause your other employees to feel anxious and stressed about the security of their position.

When an Employee Steals

Theft by their own employees accounts for 30 percent of losses suffered by small businesses. How would an employee steal from a law firm? An employee can steal cash payments made by clients. An employee can directly steal company supplies and postage. An employee can adjust or write off a client's bill and then pocket the money when it is paid in full.

The ingenuity of a determined thief is insurmountable; however, you can limit your losses by controlling the handling of cash and checks and instituting procedures to curtail opportunities for theft. While the handling of funds and accounting can be delegated to staff, it should not be turned over completely to a single employee. You should always know what is going on in your books and you and your accountant should regularly check the books for any suspicious activity. You should be aware of what each client owes and what has been paid to date. Sloppy record keeping will make a thief's job much easier. Instruct the person who opens your mail to immediately stamp any incoming checks with a "for deposit only" endorsement stamp. Reconcile your books monthly.

EMPLOYER CHECKLIST

Keep the following checklist near as you navigate the hiring process.

As you interview, remember to be thorough and conscientious:

- ✔ Seek out and confirm potential employees' work history. A previous employer may only reveal an employee's date of hire, date of termination, and job title, but at least you will be able to confirm that the information provided on a resumé is accurate.
- ✔ Consider conducting a background check on potential employees. A background check will supply arrest and conviction records that are public information.
- ✔ Establish interview guidelines based on the skills and experience needed for the job. Formulate open-ended questions before the interview takes places that will give you some insight into the applicant's work experience and his or her attitude towards the work environment.
- ✔ Be mindful of employment laws.
  The Civil Rights Act: prohibits discrimination on the basis of race, color, religion, sex, or national origin. It also prohibits sex discrimination on the basis of pregnancy and sexual harassment.
  The Equal Pay Act of 1963: prohibits employers from paying different wages to men and women who perform essentially the same work under similar working conditions.
  The Immigration Reform and Control Act of 1986: prohibits discrimination on the basis of national origin or citizenship of persons who are authorized to work in the United States.
  The Americans with Disabilities Act: prohibits discrimination against persons with disabilities.
  The Bankruptcy Act: prohibits discrimination against anyone who has declared bankruptcy.
  The Age Discrimination in Employment Act: prohibits discrimination against individuals who are age 40 or older.

Once you hire an employee, remember to complete all the necessary paperwork.

✔ File an Employee Eligibility Verification I-9 Form for every employee. This form must be completed within three business days of hiring an employee (the I-9 form can be found at www.uscis.gov).

✔ Have the employee complete a W-4 Form, otherwise known as Employee's Withholding Allowance Certificate. As an employer, you are required to withhold income taxes from an employee's wages based on the employee's marital status, amount of wages earned, and the number of withholding allowances selected by the employee. If you do not have a W-4 for an individual, you are required by law to treat the employee as a single person with no exemptions for withholding purposes. The W-4 can be found at www.irs.gov.

✔ You must pay payroll taxes. Consider using a payroll tax service such as www.PayCycle.com, which is designed for small business owners. This program automates tax reporting and payroll, which is imperative to maintaining accurate financial records. Programs offering such services typically charge $14.99 to $42.99 per month, depending on the level of service needed.

✔ Keep in mind, the IRS requires employers to maintain payroll and employment tax records for four years, including the name, address, and Social Security number for each employee; the total amount and date of each payment; the portion of each payment that constituted taxable wages; copies of each employee's W-4; date and amounts of tax deposits; and copies of returns you filed.

THE MISNOMER
OF BALANCE

*"Learn some and think some and draw and paint
and sing and dance and play and work every day some."*
—*Robert Fulghum*

Balance does not exist. It is the holy grail of the attorney.

Balance is synonymous to a scale of justice. Even if the scales appear balanced for a moment, it only takes a little pressure to make one side rise above the other. The scales are constantly adjusting and realigning themselves based on the pressure they receive.

As a solo practitioner, although it now may be easier to attend your child's school play or coach little league baseball, those brief moments of retreat from the office are often followed by a Friday night hunched over your desk at 10:00 p.m. to catch up on what was missed when you were away. You have attained the ability to make choices. You now can determine what is most important at that moment in time. There will be days when one scale tips to one side and the other side must relent. There will be days when the scales teeter, each vying for your attention. As a solo practitioner, the risk of becoming a "workaholic" is great as there is always something that needs to be faxed, e-mailed, or drafted. There is also the risk of allowing too much free time into your schedule so that clients feel neglected and unimportant.

When your life is consumed by your work, you are left with little time for your family and yourself. When work takes second chair to your personal life, your practice's growth stifles. The challenge is knowing when to focus on what in your life so that both your personal and professional lives thrive. Your goal should not be necessarily to live a balanced life, but rather to live a fulfilled life—both personally and professionally.

JUGGLING FAMILY AND WORK...
MISSION IMPOSSIBLE (OR POSSIBLE?)

If you ever had to close a sale quickly so you could scramble to daycare before it closes, pick up the dry cleaning, purchase groceries, prepare dinner, wash the dishes—all before your daughter's seven o'clock piano lesson, you understand the challenge of juggling.

Attaining work-life balance is especially difficult for the solo practitioner because his or her career is more than just a job—it's a calling. The profession is in limbo between two schools of thought: applauding unlimited devotion to work to win the big case or make partner compared to an attorney's desire to enjoy and appreciate personal relationships and life outside of the law. American Bar Association Past President Robert Hirshon probably said it best in the preface to *Balanced Lives: Changing the Culture of Legal Practice* (The ABA Commission on Women in the Profession, September 2001). He wrote:

> Most of us were attracted to the law for the nobility of its principles; the rule of law and the peaceful resolution of disputes that is so essential for any society to flourish. But, if we endeavor to be a positive force in our nation's progress, we must also be good parents and good spouses, good friends and good neighbors. We must uplift those less fortunate. A lawyer, after all, is also a citizen. The noble life is a life of balance, with each obligation attended to. No responsibility should be completely sacrificed for the benefit of another.

To attain balance, attorneys need to make peace with imperfection—a daunting task as we tend to be perfectionists by trait. Not every client needs to schedule a Saturday morning appointment and not every dinner needs to homemade. What is important is not always what is urgent. And what is urgent is not always really that urgent. Most things we put on our "to do" lists need not be done at all. When you can, outsource whatever can be outsourced. Hire a professional to clean your house. Hire a landscaper cut the lawn. Be picky about the parties you select to attend. The lesson: Do not neglect the important things in your life, that is, family and friends, for the little things that add up to a lot of nothing.

To reach fulfillment, we must recognize that our professional and personal life each must be sacrificed at times. There is not enough of you to go around all the time so you must choose what is a priority at that moment in time. When you make the right choices for the right moments, you are on your way to living a fulfilled life.

Life is too short to abandon the pleasures in life. Finding congruence between work and your family life is not impossible, but it does take a conscious effort.

THE "DO" LIST

The biggest obstacle to attaining work/life balance is yourself. We tend to not allow ourselves to relax or to unwind. The following are a few tips to keep in mind as you strive to find fulfillment equally in both your personal and professional life.

- **Do Be Selfish.**

Although I do not believe that time spent on purely your own well-being is actually "selfish-time," it is often how we feel when we decide to dedicate a moment, no matter how brief, to do something that only benefits ourselves. The benefits of making your own schedule and gaining flexibility through self-employment are only benefits if you utilize them.

Schedule two hours a week of "selfish time" like you would any other appointment and do not cancel it. It can be whatever you would like it to be. Leave your spouse at home. Leave your children in daycare. Leave your electronic devices in the glovebox of your car. Spend these two hours per week being gloriously selfish.

- **Do Establish Clear Priorities.**

Think about the choices you make on a daily basis. Many people do what is expected of them, rather than what they want to do. Priorities need to be set and reassessed on a regular basis. Your priorities may change at different points in your practice and your personal life. Are you networking effectively? Has monthly billing become a bi-monthly task? Assess what has faltered in your practice and personal life, and commit to making sure these things become a priority again.

- **Do Learn How to Turn Your Cell Phone Off.**

You will not be able to leave work at work once you decide to open your own business. Your BlackBerry® will vibrate on a Sunday afternoon while you are debating which cereal to buy in Aisle 2 of the supermarket. You will immediately stop mid-selection and ignore the glares of other shoppers to respond to a potential new client's e-mail because she is begging for a consultation at 9:00 a.m. on Monday and that could be a new client, a new retainer, a new referral base.

Do not be afraid to leave your phone on the nightstand, in the glovebox, or off. Clients are people and most of them do not expect an immediate reply to an e-mail that is sent out on a Saturday night at 10:00 p.m. And those that do, you probably do not want as clients anyway. Although modern technology makes practicing from anywhere that much more convenient, it also makes it more difficult to separate work from personal time. Give yourself permission to turn your phone off.

- **Do Call in Backup.**

Compile a list of people who you can call in a crunch. This list should include personal (family, relatives, babysitters, neighbors) contacts for personal emergencies as well as business contacts for situations that may arise at work. A snow day at your child's school can invoke panic in even the most stoic individual if you have a trial scheduled for the same day that is proceeding despite the snow. Do not be afraid to ask for help. Many people are more than willing to help if only they are asked.

- **Do Plan Vacations and Take Them.**

A vacation does not need to be an elaborate African safari. It can be simply a weekend away in a ski chalet or a few days at the beach. It is important to re-charge mentally and physically, and just being away from your commute and the ringing phones and demanding clients is what the doctor ordered. Plan vacations during slow times for your business.

...AND ONE DON'T

Don't be afraid to say "no." You cannot please everyone. You cannot be everywhere at one time. You cannot be a superstar attorney, superstar volunteer, and superstar parent. Turn down the request to spearhead the community center yard sale. Regretfully decline the invitation to co-chair a local bar association committee that you know will require you to participate in bi-weekly luncheons. It is okay to not only say "no," but to also not feel guilty about saying "no."

STRONG BODY, STRONG MIND

Resilience is defined as the ability to withstand pressure and emerge even stronger. Your business is going to give rise to daily challenges. You need to be able to handle challenges by training your body to be strong both physically and mentally. The Centers for Disease Control and Prevention reports that chronic diseases, such as heart disease, cancer, and diabetes, are the leading causes of death and disability in the United States with cardiovascular disease being the number one killer. These chronic diseases account for 70 percent of all deaths in the United States, which is 1.7 million each year. These diseases also cause major limitations in daily living for almost 1 out of 10 Americans or about 25 million people. Although chronic diseases are among the most common and costly health problems, they are also among the most preventable. Prevent health problems before they appear. Adopting healthy behaviors such as eating nutritious foods, being physically active, and avoiding tobacco use can prevent or control the devastating effects of these diseases. Go to the doctor on a regular basis and have your cholesterol checked, vision and hearing tested, blood pressure screened, skin inspected, body fat analyzed, and so forth. Equally destructive are the harmful physical and emotional effects of stress that can lead to poor health and even injury. Changing jobs and redefining your financial situation are significant life changes that prompt stress. In addition to the stress of operating a business and practicing law, you will also need to adjust your personal finances and time management skills. Research has shown that job performance decreases more rapidly as stress increases. When stress is not addressed nor alleviated, burnout ensues, which is a state of exhaustion that stems from long-term stress. The physical factors of stress can be both immediate as well as long-term when stress is continuous. See Figure 11.1 for a list of immediate and long-term physical effects of stress.

Immediate Physical Effects	Long-Term Physical Effects
Increased Heart Rate	Heart Attack
Increased Blood Pressure	Stroke
Increased Blood Glucose	Hypertension
Blood Clotting	Increased Cholesterol
Allergies	Ulcers
Skin Rashes	Weakened Immune System

Figure 11.1. A list of immediate and long-term physical effects caused by stress.

The psychological effects of stress can be just as damaging as the physical. Figure 11.2, on the next page, provides a list of some psychological effects.

Exercising and rest are paramount to achieving physical wellness. Despite the many benefits of exercise, statistics show that two-thirds of American adults are not physically active on a regular basis and a quarter get virtually no exercise at all. Why? The most common reason cited is a lack of time, fitness experts say. Schedules are overbooked and things like exercise often aren't a high priority.

Psychological Effects
Tension and Anxiety
Fatigue
Feelings of Defeat and/or Hopelessness
Agitation
Restlessness
Increased or Decreased Food Consumption
Increased Use of Unhealthy Products such as Cigarettes, Alcohol, Prescription Drugs, and Illegal Substances

Figure 11.2. A list of psychological effects of stress.

The American College of Sports Medicine (ACSM) and the American Heart Association (AHA) recommend the following:

✔ Do moderately intense cardiovascular activity 30 minutes a day, five days a week;

OR
✔ Do vigorously intense cardiovascular activity 20 minutes a day, 3 days a week;

AND
✔ Do 8–10 strength-training exercises, 8–12 repetitions of each exercise, twice a week.

Moderate-intensity physical activity means working hard enough to raise your heart rate and break a sweat, yet still being able to carry on a conversation. It should be noted that to lose weight or maintain weight loss, 60 to 90 minutes of physical activity may be necessary. The 30-minute recommendation is for the average healthy adult to maintain health and reduce the risk for chronic disease. When you exercise, your body benefits both emotionally and physically. The emotional and mental benefit of exercise stems from morphine-like chemicals that are produced in the area of the brain called the thalamus. These chemicals, called endorphins, are associated with a state of euphoria often called a "runner's high." Rest is equally as important as exercise. Without enough rest, your concentration declines, stress increases, and your energy takes a dive. Exercise makes it easier to rest and being well rested gives you the energy to exercise.

You only get one body. Treat it kindly, so you can work and play hard.

THE TROUBLED ATTORNEY

Statistically, lawyers are rated as the profession most plagued with depression, alcohol and drug addiction, and stress-related illness. Alcoholism, substance abuse, and depression affect the life of the impaired attorney, his family, the quality of professional services rendered to clients as well as the societal image of the profession.

The troubled attorney emerges from law school idealistic about his future and career path. He is determined to help others, but as his career advances, feelings of alienation, inadequacy, and hopelessness persevere. While concern for client satisfaction climbs the priority list, concern for his own life plummets along with his sense of control. Consequently, he feels overwhelmed and overworked and turns to substance abuse to alleviate the pressure or sinks into a debilitating depression. Alcohol and drug addiction is a disease that, if left untreated, can be fatal and cause untimely death.

Society has stigmatized individuals who use drugs. Often drug abusers are labeled immoral or weak. One common belief is that drug abusers should be able to just stop taking drugs if they are only willing to change their behavior. What people often underestimate is the complexity of drug addiction. Drug abuse is not simply a matter of willpower, but rather addiction is a mental illness. Addiction changes the brain by disturbing a person's normal hierarchy of needs and desires and substituting new priorities connected with obtaining and using the drug. The resulting compulsive behavior that overrides the ability to control impulses is similar to other mental illnesses.

Likewise, major depression is a serious medical illness affecting 9.9 million American adults, or approximately 5 percent of the adult population, in a given year. Studies have shown that lawyers are at a higher risk for developing the illness of depression. Male lawyers in the United States are two times more likely to commit suicide than men in the general population, according to a 1992 study by the National Institute for Occupational Safety and Health. Those who suffer from perfectionism are at higher risk for suicide. They are driven by an intense need to avoid failure. To these people, nothing seems quite good enough, and they are unable to derive satisfaction from their personal or professional life.

Major depression can significantly interfere with an individual's energy level, memory, and ability to focus and think clearly. Depression affects behavior, mood, activity level, and physical health. Depression can torment a suffering individual for years, and if left untreated, can lead to suicide.

Alcohol and drug abuse have had a significant impact on the attorney disciplinary system in which substance abuse and disciplinary actions are closely linked. The legal profession has acknowledged and addressed this problem by offering programs to help attorneys conquer the illness. Every state offers confidential programs that provide supportive structure for recovery from chemical dependence and mental health disorders. The typical program offers educational services, diagnosis, intervention, and treatment via group and individual meetings facilitated by licensed mental health professionals. The lawyer assistance programs also offer assistance with after-care and recovery. Attorney assistance programs are usually free. Education and support can make all the difference to recovery and the resumption of the attorney's life.

As solo practitioners, we can lead the march towards healthy and balanced practices and lives. We can be a positive presence in both the lives of those we serve and the lives of those we tuck into bed each night. Strive for a life of quality rather than quantity of wealth accumulated. At the end of your life, memories matter, not material objects.

12

TIPS AND MISTAKES

"Success is not final, failure is not fatal: it is the courage to continue that counts."
—*Sir Winston Churchill*

50 TIPS TO A SUCCESSFUL PRACTICE

There is no magic formula or secret to building a successful practice, but rather it is built upon perseverance, dedication, and passion for personal and professional fulfillment. The following are tips—some practical, some philosophical—as you embark on the journey of entrepreneurship. While some tips are exclusive to the legal profession and some tips are exclusive to the business owner, others are just words of encouragement as you plunge into the exhilarating experience of starting your own business. Adversely, common mistakes that attorneys make can be so severe as to be the demise of their practice. Sometimes the mistakes are intentional, but more often than not, they are the result of unintentional conduct due to poor office management.

As stated by Confucius, "Our greatest glory is not in never falling, but in rising every time we fall."

1. When Things Get Tough, Keep Going.

No one learns to ride a bike without earning a couple minor scars. When you first learned to ride, you fell over and over again. You scraped your knee and shed a few tears, but you got up, brushed yourself off, and tried again until you eventually learned how to keep the bike upright and cruise around the driveway on your own. Look at your new practice through the eyes of a six-year-old learning to ride a bike. Instead of giving up when you hit a bump in the road, learn from each bump, dust yourself off, and keep going.

2. Get and Stay Organized.

Keep a running "to do" list that is organized into what needs to be done, should be done, and can wait. Update this list frequently and check each item off as you complete the task. Get a hand-held device and sync it with your office computer so that your schedule is always at your finger tips. Designate time each day to sort through your mail and return phone calls so that neither task gets overwhelming. Being organized is also the key to reducing and managing stress.

3. Have a Disaster Plan.

Disasters can be the demise of your business if you do not have different plans in place for different situations. There are three types of disasters: medical, natural, and financial. Maintain a reliable list of people whom you can call on to help you in a bind. If your child is sick or school is closed due to the weather, do you have a babysitter or family member you can call? Establish a short list of attorneys whom you can call on in a crunch to cover a court appearance.

Secure disability insurance in case you are unable to work long-term. Although many insurance companies require at least two to three years of earning history to determine eligibility, there is insurance out there for start-up business owners.

You also need a plan for disasters of a different nature. What if your office were to burn down while you were sleeping? Make sure all of your computer programs and data are backed up and stored at an off-site location.

Lastly, it takes awhile to generate revenue and if you are profitable in your first or second year, that is a gift. Therefore, plan accordingly and make sure you have enough personal finances saved to live on when you start to avert a financial disaster.

4. Be Confident in Your Abilities.

If you are confident in your abilities, then others, whether they are clients, opposing counsel, or judges, will listen a little closer to what you have to say. Do not let more experienced attorneys intimidate you just because they have more years under their belts. You are an attorney just as they are and your voice can be just as strong. Body language speaks volumes about your confidence level so stand up straight, speak clearly, and maintain eye contact. When you fidget, lower your eyes, mumble, and hunch your shoulders, you are telling the other person, loudly and clearly, that they should doubt your abilities and what you are saying. Even if you don't feel confident, fake it.

5. Don't Compare Yourself to Others.

Our egos can create inner turmoil. If you are constantly comparing yourself, your business, and your client book to others, you allow the world around you to control how you feel about yourself. Rather than compare yourself to your colleague in the shared office space, compare yourself to yourself. Look at how much you have accomplished and how you have grown as an attorney, business owner, and individual. It is harder to acknowledge your own self-worth than it is to compare yourself to everyone else, but once you do, you will feel more inner peace, personal power, and positive energy in your life.

6. Stay Educated.

If there was a new medical treatment available to treat an illness you have, wouldn't you want your doctor to know about it, as well as its risks and benefits? Likewise, you should stay abreast of new laws by attending continuing legal education classes. Instructors usually provide their contact information to attendees, so this is another good way to build a core network of attorneys whom you can call upon with questions.

7. Think Logically.

Make decisions rationally and based on fact. Emotions have no place in your business. Don't misunderstand this to mean you cannot show compassion and empathy for clients, but rather make business decisions after careful thought and consideration and after you understand the impact they will have on your business. Business is business and you need to operate that way.

8. Always Be Straightforward, Communicative, and Ethical.

The reputation you build in this profession will remain with you for the duration of your career. Clients will appreciate straightforward communication as well as prompt and responsive communication. In the same respect, do not make promises that you cannot keep. Never promise a particular outcome and do not promise to do something for a client if you know you will not have time this week to accomplish that task. Remember, happy clients may never mention your name to anyone, but unhappy clients will spit your name to everyone they know.

9. Be Frugal.

One lucrative month does not mean a pass to splurge. Do not make expensive personal or business expenditures just because you had a couple profitable months. The subsequent months could just as easily be slow. Expand your business slowly and intelligently; that is, only after your budget is reviewed, analyzed, and revised to fit your future plans.

10. Do Not Take It Personally.

Clients sometimes are unhappy with us. It is the nature of the business. You need to be your client's effective advocate, not a best friend. Sometimes that means telling your client things that are hard to hear. It is far worse to expect success and walk away disappointed than to be prepared for the worst and walk away satisfied with the outcome.

11. Diversify.

Do not put all your eggs in one basket. Do not allow any client to make up more than 20 to 25 percent of your business. Even though a high-paying client may be able to sustain your business, this client will also likely demand most of your attention and dictate your profitability. If the client should decide to take business elsewhere or legal matters resolve, you could be left with very little income.

12. Know Your Numbers.

A common tale among solo practitioners is the one about the employee who stole from them. Often bookkeeping is the last task we want to be doing ourselves and often attorneys delegate this role to an employee, whether part-time, full-time, or a sub-contractor. Get a handle on the numbers. It is critical to understand the financial side of your business. You will be more likely to catch a pilfering employee if you know what is going on in your books. Ask questions, ask for help, but do not pass the buck on this task.

13. Send out Invoices on Time, All the Time.

Clients will not call you to ask if they owe you money. If you do not send out monthly invoices, your chances of getting paid are slim. It is easier to get a client to pay smaller monthly bills than a large bill that has accumulated over several months. Likewise, clients will appreciate a statement showing the time spent on their file. If you discounted the bill at all, make sure you make a notation of the discount on the invoice so the client feels like they received more for their money.

14. Put Clients on the Spot.

Do not be afraid to call clients to ask for payment. If you have not received payment within 30 days of sending an invoice, call the client on day 31. Often a personal phone call will shame a client into paying his or her bill. If you simply resend the bill, the client will likely slip it into the kitchen junk drawer where your previous bill still sits.

15. Act with Integrity.

It is possible to have a thriving practice while also maintaining your core values. Integrity is everything. If your client asks you to do something you are not comfortable with, explain that in written correspondence. As an attorney, you are not a puppet and your client the puppeteer. When you allow a client unfettered control of a case, your reputation and—in extreme cases—your license are at stake. You worked hard to earn that "esq." tailing your name. Treat it with the respect it deserves.

16. Acknowledge Your Flaws.

It's important to recognize your flaws, so you can address them. Attorneys who appreciate their shortcomings can be sure that these flaws never become a hindrance to productivity or the demise of their practice.

17. Be Prepared.

There is no excuse for lack of preparation. Ever. Always show up for court on time and prepared. Bring copies of motions and briefs to court in case the court cannot locate the copy that was filed. Know the facts of your case and know your client. Attention to detail is a trait that sets a great attorney apart from a mediocre attorney.

18. Always Pay Vendors on Time.

You never know when you may need one of these people to provide services quickly. A marshal who is consistently paid on time will be more willing to immediately serve that summons and complaint whose statute of limitations has nearly run. A printer whose invoice was paid immediately will probably expediently fill your order for more letterhead when you are down to your last sheet.

19. Laugh.

Although laughter will not reconcile your bank records or reverse a court's adverse ruling, laughter can (a) improve mental functioning, (b) exercise and relax muscles, (c) improve respiration, (d) stimulate circulation, (e) decrease stress hormones, (f) increase the immune system's defenses, (g) increase pain threshold and tolerance, and (h) increase personal satisfaction. Most of the things you worry about will probably never become a reality, and what seems like a huge problem today you may not even remember a few years from now. So relax a little, lighten up a little, and laugh a little.

20. Build Relationships with Other Professionals.

Bankers, accountants, financial advisors, physicians, chiropractors, realtors—they can all be a good referral source. Maintain regular contact with these people so that when the times come, they remember you. Send personal notes, plan lunch meetings, pick up the phone to say hello. Once you identify a network of contacts, keep the relationships fresh. The time and energy put into these relationships is minimal compared to the benefit that each of you can offer to the other.

21. Delegate.

This may be one of your hardest tasks yet, because most attorneys I know do not want to release their grasp of a case. If your workload becomes overwhelming, be grateful, then delegate. Even if you cannot afford to bring on a full- or part-time employee, now may be a great time to use a sub-contractor on a per diem basis. You can expect to pay anywhere from $25 to $50 per hour to pay a paralegal to draft motions, prepare discovery, and compose complaints. Less time you spend doing "busy work" means the more time you have to focus on bringing in new work.

22. Remember to Pay Yourself.

Cut yourself a check every week for the same amount. Factor it into your budget just as you would one of your other operating expenses. Open a business savings account to begin accruing a safety net from which to draw if you need to cover expenses or to assure that you are paid each week.

23. Toot Your Own Horn.

Whether you want to believe it or not, you are a salesperson. You must sell your services to every potential new client. You must make the new client believe that you are the knowledgeable, competent, and passionate attorney that you actually are.

24. Do Not Guess.

You are not supposed to have all the answers, all the time. If a client poses a question that you do not have an answer to, explain that you would like to research the issue and get back with an answer. The client will appreciate your candor and will appreciate a correct answer, rather than a shot in the dark.

25. Write Everything Down.

You cannot remember everything. You will be thankful you documented every phone conversation if you are ever grieved. You may recall that you spoke to a particular client every other day for three months, but if you did not keep track of these phone conversations, you will not be able to produce a phone log to dispute the client's assertion that you rarely returned her phone calls.

26. Slow Down.

It is just as important to build leisure time into your life. Otherwise, you risk burning out, which equates to less productivity. Play should be an outlet for stress, not yet another source of stress.

27. Be Social.

Join associations, volunteer for membership committees, and then attend events held by these groups. The associations do not need to be strictly professional. By joining a book club, you can network with people whom you may have never met otherwise. Volunteering for a community fundraiser may help foster relationships outside of your professional circle. Join a cycling group because you relish the time outdoors. You will be surprised how many referrals you will get just by doing something you enjoy with people whose company you enjoy.

28. Build a Team.

Establish a network of colleagues whom you trust and can turn to for brainstorming, advice, and guidance. I have friends who just happen to be attorneys. I will not hesitate to ask them a "stupid" question or ask their opinion on a case. It helps if each friend practices in a different area of law. For example, I have a friend I turn to for all probate and real estate questions. I have another friend I turn to when I need to value a personal injury case and yet another for all my criminal law questions.

29. Trust Your Gut.

Do not underestimate the power of your intuition. If you have a hunch that a potential new client may not be forthright with you, follow your gut and turn down the case. However, when making business decisions base them on logical and rational thinking, not hunches.

30. Adapt to Change.

You must either change with times or be left behind. When your local court starts implementing e-filing, use it. Although Internet marketing has not entirely replaced more traditional advertising, it can be a significant source of client contact. Have a Web site designed by a professional and blog regularly. Technology allows greater freedom from your office. Get a hand-held device and sync it with your office computer, so you can receive e-mails, make appointments, and bill your time when you are on the road or at home.

31. Deal with Problems.

A problem will not go away if you ignore it. Do not think that if you avoid calling back the client then you will not need to tell about the unfavorable decision that the court rendered. A missed filing date is a missed filing date. Do not pretend that it did not happen. You must notify the client as soon as you realize your mistake. Problems will only fester and grow, so deal with them immediately to put them behind you and move on.

32. Be Humble.

Just because you can stand in the "attorney's only" line when walking into a courthouse, does not mean you are better than anybody else. You worked hard to get through law school but many people work hard in their jobs. Your job does not make you more important than the next person. Treat people with respect and be grateful for those who put their faith in you. They are the people who give you a reason to go into work every day.

33. Reassess Your Business Regularly.

Review your business goals and objectives quarterly. Are you attending enough networking events or did your enthusiasm for these functions fade with the season? Are your efforts to consistently bill your time slipping? Perhaps you have not been sending out your monthly invoices every month. Assess what you have let lapse and make sure these things become a priority again.

34. Fight Procrastination.

Procrastination is a mechanism for coping with the anxiety or stress of completing a task or making a decision. When one procrastinates, it typically results in additional stress, guilt, and loss of productivity. These feelings can promote further procrastination until the individual has no choice but to deal with the task at hand, at which point the stress and anxiety to complete such task is that much more heightened. Why put yourself through all of that? Just do what needs to be done as soon as it crosses your desk. The best way to deal with boring or routine tasks is to do them one after another. One you get started, you will move quickly from one task to another, and at the end of an hour, you will feel like you accomplished something.

35. Maintain Discipline.

Just because you are your own boss, does not mean you have permission to sleep until 10:00 a.m. every day. Get up and get out. Whether you are going to an office outside or across the hallway to a home office, set a schedule for yourself and stick to it.

36. Learn from Mistakes.

You can only learn from your own mistakes by actually admitting that you made a mistake to begin with. Do not blame others for something you did or did not do. Owning your mistake moves you towards understanding why it was made and what can be done to avoid a repeat occurrence. Mistakes and negative experiences can sometimes be even better than successes, because you have an opportunity to learn something that a success could never teach you. Whenever you have a negative experience or made a mistake, ask yourself: What is the learning opportunity in this experience? Challenges make you a stronger attorney. Losses make you a wiser attorney.

37. Give Back.

Take one to two pro bono cases per year. Most state bar associations have a pro bono program that will screen cases and filter them to willing attorneys. As a new attorney, these cases will afford you the opportunity to start "practicing." As a more seasoned attorney, you might be reminded of the ideals that sent you to law school to begin with. As attorneys, we have a skill that should be shared equally, no matter an individual's income level. Realistically, you have a business to run and you need to make money. I am not lecturing to commit half of your practice to pro bono work, but rather, if we each take one or two cases a year, that is a lot of people we are helping just by donating our time.

38. Make Decisions and Commit to Them.

Making a decision implies that there are alternative choices to be considered. Very few decisions are made with absolute certainty, so all involve some element of risk. When faced with a decision, identify the available options and choose the one that best fits with your goals, business needs, or case strategy. The goal is to make a logical and unemotional business decision, then move on.

39. Prioritize.

Make lists in order of priority and stick to them. Some things can and will have to wait. Others need to be addressed immediately. Once you identify in which category each task falls, you lessen your chance of missing deadlines, opportunities, and productivity.

40. Stay Positive.

Take control of your attitude. If you think negatively, negative events will occur. Remember today is just a day, the week is just a week, the month is just a month. What is stressful to you today will be forgotten tomorrow. Try to remember the good, rather than focus on the bad, as we so often do in our lives.

41. Do Not Forget Your Client Is the Client.

In our role as attorneys, it is easy to lose sight of what a good result means. What it means to an attorney may be very different than what it means to our client. It is not always about winning. It is about creating the best possible situation that our client can live with at the end of the day. Compromise is often the port to such a result.

42. Find Free Advertising Opportunities.

Advertising can quickly deplete your operating account, so look for opportunities beyond the traditional phone book and newspaper venues. Volunteer to give a presentation at a local community college or Chamber of Commerce event. Write articles and submit them to both your local and national professional publications. When a reporter calls, speak to him or her, but only after formulating a few well-thought-out quotations.

43. Keep It Professional.

Clients have certain expectations of what attorneys are supposed to look like and how they are supposed to act. Dress professionally when you know you will be meeting with clients. Refrain from sharing your own personal life stories with them. Although you think it may help you connect with your clients, the fact is, your clients only care about their problems and only want to talk about their problems, especially if they are paying you by the hour.

44. Be Proud.

Take pride in your practice. Everything that leaves your office, whether it is a letter, a pleading, or a voice message is a reflection of you. Do not allow yourself to get sloppy with your work product. So long as you are proud of your practice, you will strive to offer reliable, effective, and quality representation and as a result, you will watch your business thrive over time.

45. Get Rest.

As the one and only for everything in your solo practice, you need the energy to keep on going. When your nights are restless and you are not getting adequate rest, your work gets sloppy and mistakes are made. Take care of yourself, so you can take care of your business.

46. Monitor Case Flow.

In your first year, monitor how many new cases you are getting each month to determine if there are specific months in which business is slower than other months. This will help you develop a budget for the next year. If you know that business will likely slow down during the summer months, you can adjust your budget to minimize costs during these months as well as work towards stockpiling a little extra financial cushioning so that your operating expenses do not exceed your bank account.

47. Learn to Say No.

Be careful about things you commit to. "No" is one of the hardest words for many people to say. If you want to be successful, you're going to have to learn how to say it and stick to it.

48. Eliminate Clutter.

When you have too many things on your desk or surrounding you, it can be distracting. Get control of paper chaos on your desk by only looking at a document once then discarding it, filing it, or acting upon it. Do not leave your office on Friday until your desk is cleared off and files are put away. Only keep things on your desk that are necessary. Don't leave stacks of papers piled up on the floor.

49. Envision the Future.

Where do you see your practice in five years? Would like you to purchase your own building for office space? Do you want to have an associate working for you? Write down your goals and determine what you need to acquire them. It is easy to get wrapped up in the here and now, but having long-term goals gives you vision to your future success.

50. Be Patient.

It may seem like your phone will never ring again. Have faith and then get active. You never know when you will meet your next client, so use slow time to increase your networking efforts. Attend more chamber events, more association meetings, more happy hours. Every new hand that you shake might turn into a business lead. It could take years of struggle before you are running a profitable business, but if you believe in what you do and focus on serving your clients, your business will grow.

FIVE MISTAKES THAT COULD COST YOU YOUR PRACTICE

1. Mismanaging Client Trust Accounts.

Delegation of this task is no excuse when a client trust fund is overdrawn. A solo practitioner must remain active in overseeing this function, because it could literally cost him or her the license to practice law. This account should be reconciled every month and reviewed. Keep accurate and separate records for each client—know what funds belong to which client. Never disburse a check to a client until the deposited funds have cleared. Never withdraw cash from the account, but rather always have a check as a record. Check with your state for any rules about how long account records should be maintained.

2. Failing to Have an Office-sharing or Partnership Agreement.

Think about what would happen if a partnership soured. Who would remain in the office space? Who would keep the phone lines, the Web site, the clients? A written agreement ensures that all parties know the process and consequences if the office-sharing arrangement should terminate or partnership should dissolve. Failure to address these issues in writing before they occur could be the demise of the practice you took so long to build.

3. Winging Your Cash Flow and Financial Plan.

While a budget will never be exact, especially when you first open your doors, you can estimate anticipated expenses month to month for a twelve-month period. Once you calculate your overhead, including an owner's drawer, you can determine how much revenue you need to bring in to make ends meet. If you have no concept of the money coming in and going out, you will not be able to budget your finances for the time when business slows. For example, if you know that December is going to be a slow month for you because of the holidays or a planned vacation, you can determine how much money needs to be put aside in the months leading up to December, so that your bills are paid during the slow time. Failure to forecast your finances may lead to overhead exceeding income and expenses going unpaid.

4. Forgetting to Track Your Time and Costs.

This is a simple mathematical equation. Time not billed equals fees not collected. If you are not paid, you cannot pay your own bills. If you cannot pay your own bills, your business will go under. Likewise, you should be recovering costs from the client; however, if you consistently forget to bill the expense to the client, then you are losing money. If you decide to adopt a flat-fee rate for certain matters, you should be tracking time to determine whether such an arrangement was profitable to you and to help you assess future flat-fee cases.

5. Having Sloppy Client Communications.

When a client says, "I want you to represent me," you need to have the person sign a retainer agreement before he or she leaves your office and before you do any work for the client. The retainer agreement should define your professional relationship, the scope of the matter, cost of representation, parameters and expectations of the parties, withdrawal and termination rights, and procedure. See Appendix B for client retainer forms.

When there is no retainer agreement, the client controls the terms of the relationship and you open yourself up to potential disciplinary sanctions.

Likewise, just because you know what is going on in a particular case does not mean the client does also. Failure to return phone calls, explain settlements, clarify questions, and overall communicate thoroughly and adequately with clients is an additional ground for disciplinary sanctions. While failing to adequately communicate with clients may not directly cause your business to collapse, the repercussions will ripple through your practice and negatively impact your bottom line. Malpractice insurance premiums increase. Client satisfaction decreases, resulting in unpaid bills, no referrals, and no repeat business.

13

LIPSTICK IN A BRIEFCASE: THE FEMALE SOLO PRACTITIONER

"A woman's place is in the House—the House of Representatives."
—Bella Abzug

Pushy.
Aggressive.
Overbearing.
Arrogant.

These are adjectives flung at women who market themselves much in the same way as a colleague of the opposite gender would. I once had a male colleague describe me as "ambitious," a seemingly innocuous word; however, the statement that followed was, "You don't want to marry a girl like that. She has her own agenda." Ironically, the same ambition that propelled that particular attorney to a successful career is the same ambition that marks a woman with a scarlet letter.

How does lipstick find a place in politics? "You can put a lipstick on a pig, it's still a pig," Barack Obama orated at one his speeches during the 2008 presidential election.

That sentence sparked a debate among the presidential candidates. Was Obama being sexist, like John McCain's campaign contended, or was Obama just using a common expression for trying to dress up something bad, meaning Sarah Palin's policy? The saying "lipstick on a pig" actually is a phrase commonly used in the car sales industry to describe a "hunk of junk" that is given a fresh coat of paint and then sold for full price. The expression became commonly used in the political arena to describe an old, bad policy that has been repackaged and presented as a new, innovative policy; yet, in this instance, it was being used to describe a woman...or was it? The gender card was being played.

Although society is becoming more comfortable with women assuming positions of power, traditional stereotypes about women persist. The media often focuses on trivial aspects of women in power, such as how they dress and whether they are wearing high heels. During the 2008 presidential election, how often did you hear the media discuss Barack Obama or John McCain's wardrobe? In contrast, how often was a segment done on Sarah Palin or Hillary Clinton's wardrobe? Palin's custom-fitted wardrobe and Clinton's plunging neckline each headlined the news at one point. These women did not have less substance, but the media often focused on looks and appearance, which in turn fostered stereotypes that shaped expectations and set limitations.

I recall working as an associate for a small firm early in my career. A client not only disregarded my words, but demanded that he would rather speak to "the male attorney."

My advice was discarded—the same advice given by my male counterpart, not just accepted, but welcomed. Apparently, the client needed to hear it in a baritone voice.

"Don't let it stop you," advises Attorney Coach L. Kay Wilson. Attorney Wilson, an experienced litigator and now coach to female attorneys, executives, and business owners (www.KayWilsonCoaching.com), encountered many epithets along the way. "I just didn't care what adjectives were thrown my way," she states. "My goal was to be an effective attorney for my clients and that meant pushing for their interests to be served. Part of maturing as a female attorney is to get beyond the possible names people will call you for doing your job and focus on doing the job."

Some women are not afforded the same presumption of competence as their male counterparts. Sometimes hard work alone will not yield the respect you deserve. As a female solo practitioner, you need to learn how to hold your own, use your power to promote your client's interests, and effectively promote your talents and skill sets. The success of your business and career depend on it.

THE STATISTICS

The numbers speak for themselves. They do not speak kindly, but they speak loudly, about the special challenges women face in their legal careers.

✔ Women constitute 30 percent of American lawyers.

✔ A 2000 study by the American Bar Association found that women represented 50 percent of law school graduates; however, women represented only 15 percent of partners, 15 percent of judges, 10 percent of law school deans, 10 percent of corporate counsel at Fortune 500 firms, and 5 percent of managing partners at law firms.

✔ A 2006 survey conducted by the National Association of Woman Lawyers found that female attorneys earned about $20,000 less a year than their male counterparts.

✔ Another finding by the American Bar Association is that while 85 percent of all male lawyers are married, only about half of female lawyers are married. Thirty percent of the women attorneys surveyed indicated they doubted they could combine the roles of lawyer, wife, and mother.

✔ The United States guarantees no paid leave for mothers in any segment of the workforce.

✔ The United States does not require employers to provide any paid annual leave. As a result, more women work long hours, nights, and weekends.

TRADITIONALLY FEMALE

After 5,000 years of written history, it is clear than men are not superior to women, yet men have set the norms and have dominated the legal profession for centuries. Women bring their own talents and abilities to the legal profession, and while women are not better than men, they are often different.

✔ Research shows that brain chemistry and wiring is such that women react and respond to situations and people on a more personal and emotional level than males. The legal profession has been dominated by males, and yet it is readily apparent to anyone who understands the system that it is in dire need of female values.

✔ While lawyers are often depicted as being task oriented, female attorneys are also concerned with the process and the experience of the parties. The best lawyers, men included, are concerned with helping their clients navigate the legal system in a humane way. The old paradigm of the unemotional male attorney is giving way to a new model of counseling that includes helping clients cope with their choices, not just make them.

✔ Psychological studies indicate that the average woman thinks about and values relationships more than the average man. Women tend to acknowledge other people's emotions as we speak to them. I always found it fascinating how clients, both men and women, felt comfortable enough to express emotion and cry in my office during initial consultations as they spoke about their problems. When I compared notes with male divorce attorneys, few had the same experience.

✔ On the other hand, studies indicate that increased testosterone in men is displayed through aggression, competition, self-assertion, and self-reliance. Males are programmed, more so than females, to compete to win, sometimes disregarding the costs. Differences in the way females and males communicate are also evident by their verbal conduct. Research has shown that men are responsible for 98 percent of all interruptions in everyday conversations. Why is this important? As a female attorney, this information can prepare you for situations in which you are being disrespected by interruptions from opposing counsel during your arguments or presentations to the court. If you allow your male colleague to continuously interrupt you in court, you will be less effective and your client may think you are getting bullied.

✔ "Create a record and ask the judge to intervene," advises Attorney Coach L. Kay Wilson, by saying, "May the record reflect that opposing counsel is interrupting my argument? Your Honor, please instruct Attorney Brown to stop interfering with my advocacy." It's that simple. Stand up for yourself and create a record so that you can protect your client.

LEVERAGE YOUR STRENGTHS

"It's business, not personal."

How often have you heard this phrase? Its commonality does not make it true. Your business is a reflection of you as a person. Connecting with people and being personal in situations where personal is traditionally not valued will help you succeed as a female solo practitioner.

The goal is to value your natural strengths, so other people will value those strengths also. Instead of working against your strength, work with it.

In order to be who we are, we need to accept who we are.

Women are good talkers and use speech to process thinking. Most men would probably enthusiastically agree. The areas of the cerebral cortex that are linked to language, judgment, and memory are packed with more nerve endings than in a man's brain. Thus, women use more words and longer sentences when we speak. We use speech to try and connect with others. When we connect with clients, we form relationships that can translate into repeat business, referrals, and other networking opportunities.

Women are good listeners. We have had a lifetime of practice. In our personal relationships, we have played the role as listener from child to adult. We listened, empathized, and advised our friends throughout our lives. Why should we repress this attribute in our careers? Use it and watch what happens. Clients will connect with you and when this happens, they will listen to you, talk to you, and promote you.

Women are good networkers. Listen. Be interested. Connect. Networking should be simple for women. We tend to complicate networking. Networking for business should not be distinct from your personal life. They are intertwined and weave in and out of all facets of your life. If you watch a woman engrossed in a conversation with another person who is telling an emotional story, the woman listener's facial expressions often mimic that of the storyteller.

Women's communication skills afford them greater ease to establish and maintain relationships with people. In this area, we have one leg up on the men. We can use these communication strengths to build our practice and client base.

SELF-PROMOTE AND STOP APOLOGIZING

The person who self-promotes typically gets the job; that is, depending on their gender. While there is a social expectation that women should be modest about their accomplishments, it is accepted and expected that men should self-aggrandize themselves. While women need to toot their own horn, they need to do it in a different way to avoid negative backlash. Again, this tactic is not about accepting stereotypes, but about stepping around the wall to reach the other side instead of trying to scale over it.

Once you listen and acknowledge what your clients' needs and goals are, you can promote yourself as the best person to help them meet their goals. This is not selling yourself in the traditional sense but rather about conveying how you can help clients meet their needs. Again, this goes back to listening to your clients and speaking with them and NOT to them.

Self-promotion does not need to sound like a sales pitch whereby you list your qualifications and accomplishments resume style. It can be as simple as saying to a prospective client: "You need to do X, Y, and Z to reach your goals. Here is how I can help you do that" or "You need someone who knows the law inside and out. I recently worked on this exact issue and had a successful result because I did the following." Let the client know that your services are valuable, how your services are valuable, and how the client can benefit from your services.

Apologize only when you have done something wrong. Women tend to apologize for our successes because we feel that our success is someone else's demise. We don't want to make someone else feel less by boasting about our triumphs. Give yourself permission to be proud of your accomplishments without minimizing its significance. To apologize otherwise is to let others know that you think you do not deserve your success.

YOU DON'T HAVE TO WEAR LIPSTICK

A woman's intelligence and skill are not diminished by the height of her heels. If a businesswoman is aggressive, autocratic, and directive, people whisper behind her back that she is a "bitch." If a businesswoman is traditionally feminine, then she does not have what it takes to run a successful business or be the boss. It is impossible to satisfactorily adapt to societal standards, because those standards are conflicted.

Women achieve power in a different way. A study of Fortune 500 companies conducted in 2003 concluded that highly successful women were using a combination of "masculine" and "feminine" styles, although most led by being more nurturing and inclusive. Women's authority and power came from their connection to people around them rather than leading those of lesser rank from a distance.

Some people will not like you. Some people would feel more comfortable if a male represented them. You are not going to change these people's minds. No matter how brilliant a job you did in representing them, they will find fault in your representation. As many people that are uncomfortable with a female representing them, there are just as many that seek out female representation.

The point: Be comfortable in your skin; whatever that means for you. Do not alter whom you are to conform to a standard. Women do not need to act like men to be successful attorneys. Likewise, women do not need to act "ladylike" to fulfill an expectation of feminine behavior. Female attorneys do not need to modify dress, behavior, and means of communication to adapt to male modes of operation. Some of the most skilled attorneys I know are authentic, vibrant, passionate, sassy women. The common thread among each is that she knows who she is, not what or who society expects her to be. If you embrace who you are, you will get noticed.

FIGHT LIKE A MALE

Ever notice how schoolchildren resolve disputes? The boys might throw a few punches in the schoolyard, but within a couple hours their hostility has simmered and they are buddies again. On the other hand, the girls will avoid confrontation but rather gossip about each other behind each other's backs, hold a grudge, and never forgive nor forget. In this respect, females should take lessons from the males. Hold your own, stand your ground, and do your job. Confront a problem immediately and head on. Part of maturing as a woman attorney is growing a thicker skin and learning to move past perceptions and dominance tactics.

DO NOT DISCOUNT YOUR SERVICES

Nationally, the average income for solo practitioners or lawyers in small firms range from $67,000 to $109,000 a year. A 2003 study by the U.S. General Accounting

Office found that women earn 80 percent of what men are paid. In the legal community, the statistics are even worse. According to a 2006 survey conducted by the National Association of Woman Lawyers, female attorneys' weekly wages amounted to 70.5 percent of male lawyers' wages. What's going on? There are several explanations. Some women are underpaid relative to their male peers in companies and law firms. Another explanation is that female attorneys in business for themselves tend to charge less than their male peers. Why are we shortchanging ourselves? Perhaps we do not want to be labeled "greedy" or "self-entitled." Perhaps we want to avoid someone asking us why we think we are worth that much money. The stereotype: Good girls do not ask. We do not ask for what we want, what we deserve, and what we are entitled to. As a solo practitioner, you have no one to blame but yourself if you do not charge the going rate for your skills and services.

It is your job to ask for money. The success of your business depends on it.

Set your fees in accordance with the going rate for your location and practice area. "Ask other male attorneys, not females, what they are charging, so that you get the real rate," advises Wilson. Do not think about what "you" are worth, but rather what "your services" are worth. See the distinction? By thinking in terms of your services rather than "you," you will be more inclined to price your services appropriately and not for less than what they are worth. Do not let the personal seep into professional pricing.

Also, do not discount your services before you are even asked to. This self-deprecating behavior inadvertently says, "I'm not worth my fees." Discounting is another way we underplay our abilities and skills rather than self-promote, and it sends a strong signal to the client that we are not really worth the money we are charging.

You should not charge less for what you do. When it comes to setting fees and getting paid for services, women tend to focus more on client's feelings and perceptions of them that negatively impact their bottom line. This thinking will assure that you will ask for less, accept less, and profit less than your male counterparts. The legal profession is a business, and you need to run your practice like a business.

"If you can't do it for yourself, think about how you are cheating your family, your children, and your estate out of money by undercharging," cautions Wilson.

FINANCIAL FREEDOM

Despite smashing through the glass ceiling in the legal community, women tend to neglect their financial security, often passing the task to a spouse. According to a study conducted in 2003 by the American Institute of Certified Public Accountants, 70 percent of women indicated that they needed help managing their finances.

The following are sobering facts about the financial future that women face:

✔ Women live seven years longer than men, on average. Often a spouse's pensions do not include a spousal survivor benefit.

✔ Unmarried older women are five times more likely to live in poverty than their male counterparts.

✔ Women will likely need more long-term care than their male counterparts.

✔ Eighty to ninety percent of women will be solely responsible for their finances at some point in their lives primarily because of divorce and longevity (National Center for Women and Retirement Research, 2006).

✔ In 2005, the average Social Security retirement benefit was 32 percent smaller for women than men.

✔ About 72 percent of women receive a monthly benefit of under $1,000 while about 68 percent of men receive more than $1,000 per month.

✔ In 2006, about 43 percent of all elderly, unmarried women receiving Social Security benefits relied on Social Security for 90 percent or more of their income.

Your financial landscape is your responsibility. As a business owner, you have grasped the reigns of your career. It is equally important to gain control over your financial future. No excuses. No passing the buck. Use a financial advisor and chart a course towards financial health via investment opportunities, retirement accounts, savings plans, and insurance. Although the following recommendations are not a substitute for professional financial guidance, think about the following so you can be financially secure and independent:

✔ Make sure you have adequate life insurance. The rule of thumb is that you should get coverage that is about 20 times your average income.

✔ If you are married, make sure that your husband has adequate insurance and that you are the owner of the policy. If you get divorced, as the owner of the policy, you still get the death benefit although you will likely be responsible to pay the annual premiums.

✔ Purchase disability insurance. While most insurance companies would like the company to be established for a few years, there are options out there for new companies.

✔ Set up and fund a retirement account. There are retirement accounts available to small businesses with few to no employees, often referred to as a "solo k."

✔ Contribute to a Roth IRA (if your income is less than $101,000 if you are single or $159,000 if you are married). The growth of the Roth IRA is tax-free if you have the account for more than five years and you wait to take the money out until after age 59 1/2.

TIPS FOR THE FEMALE ADVOCATE

Here are 11 tips for the female advocate to follow:

- Demonstrate confidence by being over-prepared
- Be assertive and definite in your responses
- Believe in your words and other people will too
- Do not be a wallflower—make your presence known
- Practice self-promotion until you are comfortable with it
- Be better than your opponent expects you to be
- Be honest, straightforward, and reliable—always
- Do not be afraid to make waves
- Do not tolerate verbal abuse from anyone—you deserve more respect than that
- If you have something to say, say it
- Do your best—learn from your mistakes—move on

Retired Supreme Court Justice Sandra Day O'Connor, 1963 graduate of Stanford Law School and the first female appointed to the U.S. Supreme Court, was offered a mere secretarial job upon her law school graduation. Years later she said, "Despite the encouraging and wonderful gains and the changes for women which have occurred in my lifetime, there is still room to advance and to promote correction of the remaining deficiencies and imbalances."

APPENDIX A

MASTER CHECKLIST FOR SETTING UP YOUR LAW OFFICE

The following checklist is not intended to be exhaustive. It should be customized to fit your needs, your niche, and your personal vision of your business.

THE PRACTICE
- Identify your niche
- Determine if you are partnering-up
- Select type of business and register with state
  - Solo
  - Partnership
  - Limited liability company
  - Professional corporation
- Select a firm name

THE OFFICE
- Determine office requirements
  - Reception area
  - Conference room
  - Library
  - Storage
  - Parking
  - Security
  - Signage
  - Lease term
  - Convenience
  - Expansion room
- Find office space
- Establish utilities
- Obtain post office box

BUSINESS PLAN AND BUDGET
- Identify start-up financing
- Draft expense plan
- Draft cash flow plan

OBTAIN INSURANCE
- Professional liability
- Health, dental, vision

- Long-term disability
- Life insurance
- General liability and property damage
- Workers' compensation

COMPLY WITH GOVERNMENTAL BUSINESS REQUIREMENTS
- Federal Employer ID Number (EIN)
- State ID Number

PURCHASE OFFICE EQUIPMENT/SUPPLIES/SERVICES
- Obtain phone numbers
- Obtain Internet service
- Obtain an e-mail address
- Obtain domain name
- Signage
- Copy machine
- Fax machine
- Computer
- Printer
- Scanner
- PDA
- Furniture
  - Desk
  - Computer station
  - Executive chair
  - Guest seating
  - Bookcase
  - File cabinets
  - Staff desk
  - Credenza
  - Wall art
  - Stand for fax, printer, or postage meter
  - Reception chairs and table
- Legal and office software
  - Word processing
  - Billing
  - Case management/docket control
  - Accounting
  - Research
  - Payroll
- Phone system

- Office supplies
- Stationery
- Announcements
- Postage equipment
- Open accounts with UPS, FedEx, Airborne, etc.
- Business credit card
- Coffeemaker
- Magazines for reception area
- Toys, coloring books, crayons to occupy children

OFFICE MANAGEMENT
- Set fee structure for firm
- Prepare retainer agreements
- Prepare intake sheets
- Notify bar of change of address
- Make sure occupational license is current

ACCOUNTING
- Open operating account
- Open client trust account
- Open business savings account
- Become credit card merchant

PERSONNEL NEEDS
- Secretary
- Legal assistant
- Receptionist
- IT support
- Accountant
- Prepare office policy manual

MARKETING
- Create Web site/blog
- Join professional associations and networks
- Send announcements to friends, family, and colleagues
- Send announcements to alumni publications and state and regional lawyer publications
- Advertise in phone books, newspaper, online legal directories

Appendix B

Sample Documents

GENERAL INTAKE SHEET

I. CLIENT INFORMATION

1. Name: _____

2. Address: _____

3. Social Security Number: _____

4. Phone (home): _____   Phone (work): _____

5. Date of birth: _____   Phone (cell/pager): _____

6. Name and number of person to contact in the event of an emergency: _____

   _____

II. EMPLOYMENT INFORMATION

7. Your occupation (if currently employed): _____

8. Your current job title: _____

9. Employer's company/business name: _____

10. Employer's name and address: _____

III. DESCRIPTION OF PROBLEM

11. Briefly describe the problem you would like to address with the attorney: _____

    _____

    _____

    _____

12. Is there any upcoming court dates for which the attorney should be made aware? If so, please

    list the date, time, and location of the upcoming court date. _____

    _____

CRIMINAL INTAKE

I. CLIENT INFORMATION

Name: _____

Address: _____

Phone (home):_____ Phone (work): _____

Phone (cell/pager): _____ E-mail: _____

Age: _____ Date of birth: _____ Social Security No: _____

Marital Status: ( ) Single ( ) Married ( ) Divorced ( ) Widow

Employer's name, address, and phone: _____

II. NATURE OF ALLEGATION

1. Date you were arrested: _____ Time of day _____ AM/ PM

2. Location of your arrest (street and/or town): _____

3. Name(s) of arresting officer(s) (if known): _____

4. Please list the charges you allegedly violated: _____

    _____

5. Date and location of your next court appearance: _____

6. Do you have a prior record? ( )Yes ( ) No

    If yes, list crimes you have been convicted _____

7. Are you currently on probation or parole?   ( ) Yes   ( ) No

8. Do you have any cases pending in any other court?   ( ) Yes   ( ) No

9. Are you an American citizen?   ( ) Yes   ( ) No

10. If you answered "no" to Question 9, do you have your green card?   ( ) Yes   ( ) No

DIVORCE/CUSTODY INTAKE

CLIENT INFORMATION

Name:_____

Address:_____

Phone (home):_____ Phone (cell):_____

Phone (work):_____ Phone (other):_____

Age:_____ Date of birth.:_____

Marital status: ( ) Single   ( ) Married   ( ) Divorced   ( ) Widow

E-mail:_____

Employer's name and address:_____

Marital Information

Your spouse's full name:_____ Date of birth _____

Date and location of marriage:_____

Your spouse's current address:_____

Have you been a resident of the State of Connecticut for the past 12 months? (Yes / No)

Are there any children of this marriage? (Yes/No) If so, please list their names and birthdates:

_____

_____

Are you paying or receiving child support for these children? (Yes / No) How much?_____

Previous Marriages

Have you been previously married? (Yes/No) If so, how many times?_____

Has your spouse been previously married? (Yes/No) If so, how many times?_____

Do you have any children from prior marriages and/or relationships? If so, please list:

_____

Are you paying or receiving child support for these children? (Yes / No) How much?_____

Employment

What is your place of business and occupation?_____

What is your current salary and how frequently do you get paid?_____

Do you have any type of retirement plan/pension plan (Yes/No) If so, what?_____

Marital Assets

Is there a marital residence? (Yes/No) If so, who owns it?_____

If the marital residence is owned, how much is the current mortgage?_____

When was the house purchased?_____How much equity exists in it?_____

Please list any other significant assets that you or your spouse owns (eg., land, condo, car, timeshare, etc):

_____

_____

Is there a joint bank account? If so, what bank?_____

Do you have your own bank account? If so, what bank?_____

Do either you or your spouse have life insurance policies? (Yes/No) If so, what is the policy limit and who are the beneficiaries?_____

Have you or your spouse ever received an inheritance? (Yes/No) If so, from whom was it received, when was it received, and for how much:

_____

_____

Divorce Assets

Are you and your spouse presently separated? (Yes/No) If so, when did that occur?_____

Do you believe there is any hope of reconciliation? (Yes/No)

Have you tried to reconcile previously? (Yes/No)

PERSONAL INJURY INTAKE

I. CLIENT INFORMATION

Name: _____

Address: _____

Phone (home): _____ Phone (work): _____

Phone (cell/pager): _____ E-mail: _____

Age: _____ Date of birth: _____ Social Security No: _____

Marital status: ( ) Single ( ) Married ( ) Divorced ( ) Widow

Employer's name, address, & phone: _____

Your job description: _____

II. INSURANCE INFORMATION

Your car insurance carrier (name and policy number):

_____

Does your car insurance have Med Pay coverage? ( ) Yes ( ) No

Your health insurance carrier (name and policy number):

_____

III. NATURE OF ACCIDENT

Date and time of the accident: _____

Location of the accident: _____

Description of the vehicle you occupied: _____

Were you the ( ) Driver ( ) Passenger ( ) Front Seat ( ) Back seat

What were the weather conditions at the time of the accident? _____

Were there any witnesses to the accident? ( ) Yes ( ) No

III. NATURE OF ACCIDENT (continued)

In your own words, please describe how the accident occurred: _____

_____

_____

_____

IV. MEDICAL TREATMENT

What physical problems do you suffer from as a result of the accident? _____

_____

Did you go to the hospital as a result of this accident? If so, where? _____

_____

Did you suffer from pre-existing injuries prior to this accident? If so, what were they? _____

_____

Have you seen any doctors for injuries sustained in this accident?   ( ) Yes   ( ) No

V. OTHER QUESTIONS

Have you lost time from work due to this accident?   ( ) Yes   ( ) No

      If so, where do you work? _____

      How much time did you lose from work? _____

Was there damage sustained to the motor vehicle you occupied? ( ) Yes   ( ) No

Have you taken photos of the damage that was sustained?   ( ) Yes   ( ) No

Have you ever been the recipient of state assistance / welfare?   ( ) Yes   ( ) No

Have you ever been in an accident prior to this occurrence?   ( ) Yes   ( ) No

AGREEMENT TO PROVIDE LEGAL SERVICES

GENERAL RETAINER AGREEMENT

CLIENT INFORMATION

Name: _____   SS #: _____

Address: _____   Phone (home): _____

_____   Phone (work): _____

_____   Phone (cell): _____

Scope of Representation:

THIS AGREEMENT is made this _____ day of _____, the year _____, by and between The Law Office of _____ and the Client. If the terms and conditions are acceptable as to this agreement to render services in this personal injury action, please sign on the last page.

1. **Authorization.** Client authorizes The Law Office of_____ to represent you in the above-captioned case, subject to this agreement and the requirements of state and federal law. Please note that this retainer does not apply to any post-judgment proceedings (e.g., appeals, etc.)

2. **Hourly Rate.** Our hourly rate for services to you will be $_____ per hour. In addition, you will be responsible for all reasonable and necessary out-of-pocket expenses we incur on your behalf, including (but not limited to) those expenses listed in Paragraph Four (4) of this Retainer Agreement.

3. **Retainer.** The Law Office of _____ requires a retainer of $ _____ to be paid by you at the time you enter this agreement. The Retainer is payable in full prior to an appearance being filed on your behalf in the court where your case is pending. The Retainer is calculated based on the time and labor reasonably anticipated to represent you in your case. The firm agrees to exert its best efforts in the preparation and trial of your case.

4. **Expenses.** Expenses are separate from and in addition to the retainer and applicable attorney's fees. Client authorizes The Law Office of _____ to incur expenses in representing client and client agrees to pay all such expenses incurred, including any and all expenses necessary to prepare this case for trial (should one be necessary). Expenses include but are not limited to: filing fees, investigation costs, witnesses, marshals, experts, consultants, physicians, transcripts, subpoenas, exhibits, diagrams, photography,

videography, reports, postage, express mail, online research, toxicology reports, and any other out-of-pocket expenses.

5. **Client responsible for Disbursements and/or Costs Regardless of Outcome.** Any and all disbursement charges or costs advanced by the Attorneys for or on behalf of the Client are reimbursable to the Attorneys *regardless* of the ultimate outcome of the case. Client will also be billed and such disbursements/costs will be due and payable upon receipt of the invoice by Client. Invoices unpaid after thirty (30) days from the date of issuance will be charged interest at the rate of _____ percent on the unpaid balance. Client may ask for a timesheet of hours for services rendered and/or of costs incurred.

6. **Secured Agreement.** The client grants The Law Office of _____lien on any matter described above or arising out of the above matter, and further agrees that said charging lien attaches to any funds realized by any settlement whether secured by Client or Attorneys.

7. **Termination of Representation.** The Law Office of _____may seek to terminate its representation of Client, after written notice, if in the firm's opinion, Client: (a) insists on pursuing a course of conduct or on making an illegal or prohibited claim, defense, or argument; (b) fails or refuses to cooperate or assist the firm; (c) misrepresents or fails to disclose important facts to the firm; (d) unreasonably fails to follow the firm's advice; or (e) fails to make any payment or deposit required by this agreement. Client may terminate the firm's representation at anytime for any reason.

8. **Consultation with experts.** Client authorizes the Attorneys the permission to refer and/or consult with any experts as may be necessary, at the discretion of the Attorneys for the proper handling of the case.

9. **Cost of Duplicating File.** Should the client request a photocopy of his or her file, or should the Client request return of his or her original file which requires a photocopy be made, the Client agrees to pay, in advance, the sum of $0.25 per page for photocopy charges.

10. **No Guarantees.** It is agreed and understood that NO PROMISES OR GUARANTEES HAVE BEEN MADE BY THE ATTORNEY(S) TO YOU AS TO THE OUTCOME OF YOUR CASE.

11. **Duty to Cooperate.** The Client shall at all times cooperate with and fully inform The Law Office of _____ all relevant information regarding the issues involved in your case; and notify the office regarding any changes of address, telephone numbers, etc., to facilitate orderly and prompt communication between the parties. Client also agrees to comply with all scheduling timetables as required by any judicial authority and understands that failing to comply with scheduling timetables may subject the client to judicial sanctions.

12. **Governing Law and jurisdiction.** This agreement shall be governed by the laws of the State of _____. Client consents to jurisdiction in the State of _____.

13. **Client Acknowledgment of Receipt of This Agreement..** This agreement represents the entire agreement regarding The Law Office of _____ representation of Client, fees, and expenses, and replaces any other written or oral agreements or communications. Client acknowledges that by signing below that Client has read this entire agreement, understands it and agrees to its terms. Client also agrees that by signing this Agreement s/he has received a copy.

Law Office of   **Client/Financially Responsible Party**

Name:_____   Name:_____

Date:_____   Date: _____

AGREEMENT TO PROVIDE LEGAL SERVICES

CRIMINAL RETAINER AGREEMENT

CLIENT INFORMATION

Name: _____   Social Security #: _____

Address: _____   Phone (home): _____

_____   Phone (cell): _____

Re: _____

THIS AGREEMENT is made this _____ day of _____, the year _____, by and between The Law Office of _____ and the client and/or a financially responsible party. If the terms and conditions are acceptable, please sign and return with the applicable retainer fee.

1. Authorization. Client authorizes The Law Office of _____ to represent you in the above-captioned case, subject to this agreement and the requirements of state and federal law.

2. Retainer. The Law Office of _____ requires a retainer of $ _____ to be paid by you at the time you enter this agreement. The Retainer is payable in full prior to an appearance being filed on your behalf in the court where your case is pending. The Retainer is calculated based on the severity of the charges, time, and labor required, the location of the court, prior record and probation status of the accused, and any other factors applicable to your case. If this case is disposed of in a manner other than by trial, no portion of the Retainer fee shall be returned to you. Note that if your case should be transferred to another court, additional financial arrangements may become necessary.

3. Expenses. Expenses are separate from and in addition to the retainer and applicable attorney's fees. Client authorizes the firm to incur expenses in representing client and client agrees to pay all such expenses incurred, including any and all expenses necessary to prepare this case for trial (should one be necessary). Expenses include but are not limited to: filing fees, investigation costs, witnesses, marshals, experts, consultants, physicians, transcripts, subpoenas, exhibits, diagrams, photography, videography, reports, postage, express mail, online research, toxicology reports, and any other out-of-pocket expenses.

4. The trial fee. If a trial becomes necessary, the trial fee is $_____ per day. We will estimate the number of trial days and will require that the amount be paid in full prior to jury selection. If the actual number of trial days exceeds the estimate, you will be responsible for the differential.

5.   Scope of representation. The firm is obligated to represent client in the case described above, and the firm will utilize professional efforts in doing so. The firm is not obligated to represent client in any retrial after mistrial or a reversal by an appellate court; proceedings involving probation, parole or other similar program; appeals, forfeitures, or a similar program. Representation in any proceeding or matter not covered by this agreement requires a new agreement signed by the firm and the client.

6.   Punctuality. The firm expects that you attend all court appearances in a punctual manner on your assigned court dates. The firm also expects that you keep all appointments made with the office. Additionally, the attorneys of this firm exert every effort to arrive punctually to court on a daily basis, however at times circumstances arise where an attorney may first be required to appear in another court. While this generally does not occur, the situation does arise at times and we ask that you understand that this could happen.

7.   No Guarantees. It is agreed and understood that NO PROMISES OR GUARANTEES HAVE BEEN MADE BY THE ATTORNEY(S) TO YOU AS TO THE OUTCOME OF YOUR CASE.

8.   Keep us informed. The client shall at all times cooperate with and fully inform the firm with all relevant information regarding the issues involved in your case; and notify the office regarding any changes of address, telephone numbers, etc., to allow for proper and prompt communication with you.

9.   Billing and interest. The Law Office of _____ may provide client with statements that detail time spent, fees and expenses. Client shall pay amounts due within fifteen (15) days. As to all sums remaining unpaid after 30 days, the client shall pay interest at the rate of five percent (5%) per month on unpaid balances; if this office must start collection efforts, client shall pay reasonable attorney's fees and the maximum amount of interest allowed by law.

10.   File retention and use. Any materials and files relating your representation are the work product and property of the firm. If all amounts due have been paid and client requests the file, the firm shall return any original materials supplied by client and provide photocopies of correspondence, pleadings, or other items at client's expense. The firm also retains pertinent material from client's file for at least three years, after which the firm may destroy the file and material without further notice.

11.   Termination of Representation. The Law Office of_____ may seek to terminate its representation of client, after written notice, if in the firm's opinion, client: (a) insists on pursuing a course of conduct or on making an illegal or prohibited claim, defense or argument; (b) fails or refuses to cooperate or assist the firm; (c) misrepresents or fails to disclose important facts to the firm; (d) unreasonably fails to follow the firm's advice; or (e) fails to make any payment or deposit required by this agreement. Client may terminate the firm's representation at anytime for any reason.

12.   **Governing Law and jurisdiction**. This agreement shall be governed by the laws of the State of _____. Client consents to jurisdiction in the State of _____.

13.   **Binding Effect.** This agreement is binding on the respective heirs, executors, legal representative, successors, and assigns of all parties.

14.   **Entire agreement**. This agreement represents the entire agreement regarding The Law Office of _____ representation of client, fees, and expenses, and replaces any other written or oral agreements or communications. This agreement can only be modified in writing and signed by both parties.

15.   **Signature.** The undersigned have read, understood, and consented to this Agreement for legal services and agree to be obligated by its terms.

Law Office of   **Client/Financially Responsible Party**

Name:_____   Name:_____

Date:_____   Date: _____

AGREEMENT TO PROVIDE LEGAL SERVICES

PERSONAL INJURY RETAINER AGREEMENT

CLIENT INFORMATION

Name: _____   SS #: _____

Address: _____   Phone (home): _____

_____   Phone (work): _____

_____   Phone (cell): _____

Date of Injury:_____

THIS AGREEMENT is made this _____ day of _____, the year _____, by and between The Law Office of _____ and the client and/or a financially responsible party. If the terms and conditions are acceptable as to this agreement to render services in this personal injury action, please sign on the last page.

1.   Authorization. Client authorizes The Law Office of _____ to represent you in this personal injury action which occurred on the date indicated above, subject to this agreement and the requirements of state and federal law.

2.   Scope of representation. The firm is obligated to represent client his/her personal injury matter, and the attorney will devote full professional ability to it. Further, the Client agrees to cooperate with the representation provided by the attorneys.

3.   Attorney's Fee. The attorney's fee in this case will be a contingency fee, pursuant to state law. It is therefore agreed that Client pay Attorney a percentage of the gross amount recovered in the event of settlement either before or after suit has begun or as a result of verdict or judgment. The percentages have been established in Section 1 of Connecticut Public Act No. 86-338 and reproduced here:

   a. 33 1/3% of the first three hundred thousand ($300,000.00) dollars;
   b. 25% of the next three hundred thousand ($300,000.00) dollars;
   c. 20% of the next three hundred thousand ($300,000.00) dollars;
   d. 15% of the next three hundred thousand ($300,000.00) dollars; and
   e. 10% of any amount in excess of one million two hundred thousand ($1,200,000.00) dollars.

4.   If no recovery. In the event of no recovery, Client shall owe Attorney nothing for services rendered, however the Client is still responsible for all out-of-pocket expenses incurred by the Attorney in the handling of his/her case. Those expenses are described in Paragraph 5.

5.   Expenses. Client agrees to pay all out-of-pocket expenses that the Attorneys incur in the course of representation, *regardless of the outcome of the case.* These expenses may include, but not be limited to, all entry fees, medical records and reports, expert fees, probate investigations, photographs, deposition costs, phone call charges, investigation costs, witnesses, marshals, experts, consultants, physicians, transcripts, subpoenas, exhibits, diagrams, photography, videography, reports, postage, express mail, online research, toxicology reports, photocopying, and any other out-of-pocket expenses. Costs incurred which remain unpaid at the time of settlement shall be deducted from the money recovered. This office will provide you with a written accounting of all disbursements.

6.   Additional fees. No other additional legal fees will be charged unless an appeal is taken by any party in a lawsuit or arbitration proceeding. This office is not required to represent you in an appeal. This retainer agreement does not cover the costs associated with an appeal.

7.   Investigation of claim. Client understands that Attorneys will investigate Client's claim, and if after concluding the investigation the claim does not appear to have substantial merit, then Attorneys have the right to cancel this agreement. If the claim does appear to have substantial merit, then the Attorneys shall institute a lawsuit and/or arbitration proceeding after all reasonable efforts to negotiate a fair and just settlement have been exhausted. We will keep you informed of the progress of your case and all negotiations and settlement offers.

8.   Termination of Representation. The Law Office of _____ may seek to terminate its representation of client, after written notice, if in the firm's opinion, client: (a) insists on pursuing a course of conduct or on making an illegal or prohibited claim, defense or argument; (b) fails or refuses to cooperate or assist the firm; (c) misrepresents or fails to disclose important facts to the firm; (d) unreasonably fails to follow the firm's advice; or (e) fails to make any payment or deposit required by this agreement. Client may terminate the firm's representation at anytime for any reason.

9.   Consultation with experts. Client authorizes the Attorneys the permission to refer and/or consult with any experts as may be necessary, at the discretion of the Attorneys for the proper handling of the case.

10.   Alternate attorney's fee. In the event that Section 1 of Public Act No. 86-338 is repealed or declared invalid, paragraph 3 of this agreement shall be deemed amended to provide for Attorney's fees of 33 1/3% of the gross amount recovered in the event of settlement either before or after suit has begun or as a result of verdict or judgment.

11.   No Guarantees. It is agreed and understood that NO PROMISES OR GUARANTEES HAVE BEEN MADE BY THE ATTORNEY(S) TO YOU AS TO THE OUTCOME OF YOUR CASE.

12.   Keep us informed. The client shall at all times (a) cooperate with and fully inform The Law Office of _____ with all relevant information regarding the issues involved in your case;

and (b) notify the office regarding any changes of address, telephone numbers, etc., to facilitate orderly and prompt communication between the parties.

13.   Governing Law and jurisdiction. This agreement shall be governed by the laws of the State of _____ . Client consents to jurisdiction in the State of _____ .

14.   Binding Effect. This agreement is binding on the respective heirs, executors, legal representative, successors, and assigns of all parties.

15.   Entire agreement. This agreement represents the entire agreement regarding The Law Office of _____ representation of client, fees and expenses, and replaces any other written or oral agreements or communications. This agreement can only be modified in writing and signed by both parties.

16.   Signature. The undersigned have read, understood, and consented to this Agreement for legal services and agree to be obligated by its terms.

Law Office of   **Client/Financially Responsible Party**

Name:_____   Name:_____
Date: _____   Date: _____

AGREEMENT TO PROVIDE LEGAL SERVICES

SOCIAL SECURITY FEE AGREEMENT

CLIENT INFORMATION

Name: _____   SS #: _____

Address: _____   Phone (home): _____

_____   Phone (work): _____

_____   Phone (cell): _____

I, _____, hereby retain The Law Office of _____ to represent me in my application for reconsideration of Social Security Disability Benefits.

As fees for legal services, I agree to pay my Attorney as follows:

> TWENTY FIVE PERCENT (25%) OF ALL RETROACTIVE BENEFITS, NOT TO EXCEED A TOTAL FEE OF $_____.

Separate from attorney's fees, I also agree to pay for any necessary costs and expenses that my attorneys may incur in the preparation and representation of my case. The amount of any costs and expenses will be deducted from the balance of the proceeds remaining after the attorney's fees have been deducted from the gross amount of any retroactive benefit.

I understand that this fee agreement is on a contingency basis and if no benefit is awarded, I will not be obligated to pay any attorney's fees. I further understand that my obligations to pay any costs and expenses is not on a contingency basis. Thus, I agree to pay any costs and expenses regardless of whether my application for reconsideration of Social Security disability benefits is approved.

I HEREBY ACKNOWLEDGE THAT I HAVE RECEIVED A COPY OF THIS FEE AGREEMENT AND THAT I AGREE TO ALL OF ITS TERMS.

Law Office of   **Client/Financially Responsible Party**

Name:_____   Name:_____
Date: _____   Date: _____

WORKERS' COMPENSATION
ATTORNEY CONTINGENT FEE AGREEMENT

CLIENT INFORMATION

Name: _____   SS #: _____

Address: _____   Phone (home): _____

_____   Phone (work): _____

_____   Phone (cell): _____

DATE OF INJURY: _____

     In consideration of The Law Office of _____ representing me in this matter, I do hereby agree as follows:

    1.   To fully cooperate with my attorney, including providing current information with regard to home and work telephone numbers and current mailing address. In addition, I agree to promptly appear, when advised, for all court hearings, depositions, pre-trial conferences, and to furnish all information and written documentation requested by my attorneys.

    2.   The attorney's fee in this case shall be computed as follows: No more than 20% of total award to client for scarring, permanent partial disability, and final stipulation. No more than 20% of any temporary total benefits or temporary partial benefits provided they are contested.

    In addition, I agree to reimburse my attorney for any expenses or disbursements made on my behalf. Such expenses may include, but are not limited to, investigation expenses, depositions, expert's reports and fees for testifying, and medical and hospital reports and records.

    3.   This agreement does not encompass the handling of an appeal either on my behalf, or on behalf of any other party, of any judgment rendered in my case. It is understood that any agreement for the Firm to represent me on an appeal shall be separate from this agreement.

    4.   I understand that I have the right to discharge my attorney at any time. However, if I decide to discharge my attorney, I agree to compensate my attorney for any services rendered prior to the date of discharge on an hourly basis, as well as any costs, expenses or disbursements incurred by my attorney. In addition, if at the time of discharge there has been an offer made in my case, such fee will not be less than the attorney's fee applicable to such offer (as set out in Paragraph 2 above), plus costs and expenses incurred by the my attorney.

    5.   I have read the foregoing and understand it.

Law Office of   **Client/Financially Responsible Party**
Name:_____   Name:_____
Date: _____   Date: _____

AUTHORIZATION TO RELEASE INFORMATION

TO: *RE:*

You are hereby requested and authorized to disclose, make available, and furnish to my attorney:

the following information that you have in your possession:

This form serves the dual purpose of being both a general authorization for the release of information and a specific authorization for the release of information protected by state and federal confidentiality laws (if applicable). I understand the information release by this consent will not be further relayed to any other person or entity without additional consent from me except to the extent that action has already been taken in reliance on it. This consent may be withdrawn by me anytime prior to the release of the above information. If not withdrawn, this consent will expire 120 days after the day on which it is signed. Note that a photocopy of this authorization shall be deemed as valid as the original.

_____   _____
CLIENT NAME   **DATE**

To Health Care Provider:

Patient Name:_____   Date of Birth: _____
                                           Date of Loss: _____
                                           Social Security No.: _____

Disclose Health Information to (Recipient)

I authorize you to disclose to the above-named recipient my health information, including but not limited to: case history, hospital records, office visit records, physician's reports and notes, nurses notes, telephone logs, physician/hospital correspondence, medical history, consent forms, x-rays or other diagnostic studies, x-ray/film reports, pathology reports, diagnostic testing reports, laboratory reports, prescriptions and/or medication history, correspondence to and from patient, physicians, other health care providers and/or insurance companies, consultations and dental records and reports and any and all billing records, including insurance payment information.

I understand that this health information may include HIV-related information and/or information relating to diagnosis or treatment of psychiatric disabilities and/or substance abuse and that by signing this form, I am authorizing such information to be disclosed.

I authorize the above health care provider to disclose the information described above to the above named recipient and I authorize the use of the information for litigation purposes, including but not limited to, sharing this information with necessary witnesses, experts, and consultants in connection with litigation.

EXPIRATION

This Authorization will expire the later of three (3) years from the date of execution or upon final disposition of the litigation.

I understand that the above-named recipient of my health information is not a health care provider or health plan covered by the federal Privacy Rule, and therefore that the information used or disclosed as described above may be redisclosed by the recipient and no longer protected by the Privacy Rule. However, other state or federal law may prohibit the recipient from disclosing specifically protected information, such as substance abuse treatment information, HIV/AIDS-related information, and psychiatric/mental health information.

I understand that I may revoke this Authorization in writing at any time, except to the extent that the above health care provider has already taken action in reliance on this Authorization.

I understand that I am not required to sign this Authorization as a condition of treatment, payment, enrollment or eligibility for benefits.

By signing below, I acknowledge that I read and understand this Authorization form and that a copy of the Authorization shall be considered as valid and effective as the original.

_____   _____
Signature of Patient or   Date
Patient's Authorized Representative

If signed by Patient's Representative, please print name and describe relationship to Patient or other authority to act:

_____   _____
Name   Date

_____
Relationship to Patient

AUTHORIZATION TO RELEASE WAGE AND EMPLOYMENT RECORDS

TO: _____ **RE:** _____

You are hereby authorized to furnish my wage/employment records to the following attorneys concerning my loss of wages or earnings as a result of an accident which occurred on

DATE:_____

_____   _____
CLIENT NAME   Date signed

1. Occupation and kind of work:

2. How long employed prior to date of accident:

3. Average number of hours per day:

4. Average number of days per week:

5. Date stopped work:

6. Date returned to work:

7. Wages or earnings before date of accident: Hourly rate: _____,
   average weekly regular pay: _____, average weekly overtime pay: _____

8. Wages or earnings after return to work: Hourly rate: _____,
   average weekly regular pay: _____, average weekly overtime pay: _____

9. If any wages or earnings were paid to employee for period during which he was out, amount paid _____ and for what period _____.

ADDITIONAL REMARKS:.

DATE OF REPLY _____

PERSON WHO REPLIED (name and title) _____

SCHOOL RECORDS AUTHORIZATION

DATE

TO: SCHOOL NAME
           ADDRESS
           ADDRESS

FROM:

RE: STUDENT NAME
           DATE OF BIRTH
           SOCIAL SECURITY NUMBER

You are hereby authorized to furnish and release to my attorneys,_____, or any representative thereof, any and all information which may be requested relative to my education, past or present, and to furnish copies of any and all records which you may have concerning me regarding or in connection with my school records. Your full cooperation with my attorneys is requested.

A photocopy of this authorization shall be as acceptable as the original. This authorization is valid for any past, present or future requests by my attorney for such information until expressly revoked by me in writing.

_____   _____
Signature of Student or   Date
Student's Parent/Guardian

If signed by Parent/Guardian, please print name and describe relationship to student or other authority to act:

_____   _____
Name   Date

_____
Relationship to Patient

LETTER OF PROTECTION

Date:

To:

Re: CLIENT NAME: _____
       Date of Birth: _____
       Social Security Number: _____

To Whom It May Concern:

I, _____, do hereby authorize The Law Office of _____ to furnish the above-mentioned provider a letter stating that I will protect my medical bill out of any successful recovery that I may receive in the above-referenced matter.

Please note that a photocopy of this document shall be deemed as valid and effective as the original.

_____
CLIENT NAME

WELCOME LETTER

DATE

PRIVILEGED AND CONFIDENTIAL
ATTORNEY-CLIENT CORRESPONDENCE

CLIENT NAME
ADDRESS
ADDRESS

RE: CASE NAME

Dear _____ :

This letter will confirm that you have retained Attorney _____ to represent you in the above referenced matter.

Please find enclosed a copy of the retainer agreement that dictates the terms of our agreement. Each month, you will receive an invoice for fees and expenses, which will be accompanied by a description of the services rendered and expenses incurred on your behalf. I require payment of these monthly invoices within thirty (30) days of billing. If full payment of the monthly invoice is not received on a timely basis, I reserve the right to withdraw from this engagement in accordance with the governing ethic rules. Any unapplied portion of the retainer will be returned to you.

Please retain a copy of this letter and your retainer agreement for your files. If you have questions with respect to the terms of our agreement, please do not hesitate to contact me.

I look forward to working with you.

Very truly yours,

YOUR NAME

CASE REJECTION LETTER

DATE

NAME
ADDRESS
ADDRESS

RE: Potential Lawsuit

Dear _____:

Please be advised that I have had the opportunity to investigate the potential for a lawsuit on your behalf. Unfortunately, at this time I do not feel that the case has sufficient merit to warrant litigation. Therefore, I must regrettably decline to accept the case.

Each individual attorney may view the same set of facts differently. Consequently, please do not allow my rejection of the case to discourage you from seeking a second opinion. The general statute of limitations in the State of _____ is _____ years. This means that a case must be filed within _____ years of the date of injury. If you should let the statute of limitations run without filing suit, then you could very well be left without any type of remedy to redress the injuries, both financial and physical, which you sustained.

Thank you for allowing us the opportunity to look into the matter, and I am sorry that I cannot be of service to you in this instance.

Very truly yours,

YOUR NAME

LETTER OF REPRESENTATION

DATE

NAME
ADDRESS
ADDRESS

RE: **Personal Injuries sustained by my client, CLIENT NAME**
        Date of accident:

Dear NAME:

I have been retained by CLIENT'S NAME to recover damages for personal injuries which occurred as a result of a motor vehicle accident on DATE. This incident reportedly occurred on STREET and CITY.

I ask that you immediately forward a copy of this letter to your insurance carrier and ask them to contact the undersigned.

Thank you for your anticipated cooperation.

Very truly yours,

YOUR NAME

IN LIEU OF APPEARANCE LETTER

DATE

ATTORNEY NAME
ADDRESS
ADDRESS

RE: CASE NAME

Dear Attorney _____:

Please be advised that this office has been retained in lieu of yours by _____ concerning the above referenced matter.

Please prepare the file for transfer at your earliest convenience. We will be happy to pay your cost advance at the time of transfer, however, please note that any and all monies collected by way of settlement and or verdict shall be held until such time as an equitable fee split is agreed upon.

Very truly yours,

YOUR NAME

MEDICAL RECORDS REQUEST

DATE

NAME OF MEDICAL PROVIDER
ADDRESS
ADDRESS

RE: **CLIENT NAME:**
        Date of Birth:

Dear Medical Records Keeper:

Your patient, CLIENT NAME, has requested that you forward me a copy of the bill for services rendered and all medical records concerning treatment of said patient. We also request that you send us copies of all records in your possession including, but not limited to, the following:

Bill	Admissions Records
Summaries	Examinations
Laboratory Data	Treatment Records
Reports of Consultants	Prescription Records
Surgical Reports	Nurse's Notes
Incident Reports	Physician Notes
All Other Records Pertaining to This Patient	

Enclosed is a medical authorization for your records. If you should need any other information, please contact the undersigned. Thank you for your attention to this matter.

Very truly yours,

YOUR NAME

Enclosure: Authorization

MILITARY SERVICE STATUS REQUEST

DATE

Defense Manpower Data Center
1600 Wilson Blvd., Suite. 400
Arlington, VA 22209-2593
Attn: Military Verification

RE: CASE NAME
      CASE NUMBER

Dear Sir/Madam:

Pursuant to the Soldiers' and Sailors' Civil Relief Act of 1940, specifically, 50 U.S.C.A. § 501 *et seq.*, please provide the current military status of the following:

NAME/ADDRESS/ SSN / DOB	NOT IN MILITARY	IN MILITARY SERVICE
NAME ADDRESS ADDRESS SSN# (if known) DOB (if known)		

_____   _____
                                      Date

A self-addressed, stamped envelope is enclosed.

Very truly yours,
YOUR NAME

NOTICE OF COURT APPEARANCE

DATE

NAME
ADDRESS
ADDRESS

RE: CASE NAME

Dear _____:

Please be advised that court is scheduled for the above matter on _____ at _____
a.m./p.m. The address of the court is _____.

Please contact my office immediately upon receipt of this letter to confirm your attendance on
that date.

Very truly yours,

YOUR NAME

NOTICE OF DEPOSITION

DATE

NAME
ADDRESS
ADDRESS

RE: CASE NAME

Dear _____ :

Please be advised that your deposition has been scheduled to take place on _____ at _____a.m./pm. Your attendance is required so please make the appropriate arrangements to be present. The deposition will take place at the following address:

A deposition is a statement made under oath. At the deposition, you must be prepared to respond to certain questions about you and your case. Opposing counsel will ask these questions. I will be present along with a stenographer.

It is important that prior to your deposition, we meet so that you are prepared and comfortable with the process. Please contact my office as soon as possible to make an appointment.

Very truly yours,

YOUR NAME

LETTER TO DESTROY FILE

DATE

CLIENT NAME
ADDRESS
ADDRESS

RE: CASE NAME

Dear   :

Many years have passed since my office has last been in touch you regarding the above matter. Even though your file has been inactive, state law requires my office to hold your file in storage for a certain amount of time before it can be destroyed.

At this time, we are now permitted to destroy the file. Before I do so, I would like to give you the opportunity to contact my office and let us know if you would like to retrieve your file.

If I do not hear from you within two weeks of the date of this letter, then I will presume that you will not be seeking any of the information contained in the file and accordingly, the file will be destroyed.

Please let me know if I can be of any further assistance to you.

Very truly yours,

YOUR NAME

*GAS MILEAGE REIMBURSEMENT CHART**

The IRS rate is currently *58.5 cents/mile* effective through December 31, 2008.

COURT LOCATION	MILES FROM OFFICE ROUNDTRIP	REIMBURSEMENT RATE
Ansonia-Milford	18.3	$10.70
Danbury	59.94	$35.06
Derby	25.42	$14.87
Hartford	114.82	$67.17
Meriden	81.24	$47.53
Middletown	101.86	$59.59
New Britain	104.5	$61.13
New Haven	39.16	$22.91
Norwalk	31.42	$18.38
Stamford	46.48	$27.19
Waterbury	60.84	$35.59

*This chart was included as an example of how to easily calculate gas mileage if you intend on passing this cost onto your clients. Enter your office location into mapquest.com to determine distance, then multiply mileage by .585. Note that IRS rates change on a regular basis so you will need to update this chart every once in a while.

GAS MILEAGE REIMBURSEMENT FORM

CASE NAME:_____

DOCKET NO:_____

DATE	ATTORNEY	DESTINATION	DESCRIPTION	MILES	AMOUNT

LITIGATION TIME RECORDS

__CASE NAME:__ _____

__DOCKET NUMBER:__ _____

DATE	HOURS	DESCRIPTION OF SERVICES

ACTIVITY CODES:

CF = Office Conference	**DR** = Draft Documents
CR = Correspondence	**LR** = Legal Research and Writing
CT = Court Appearances	**RD** = Review Documents
DE = Depositions	**TL** = Telephone
DP = Draft Pleadings	**TV** = Travel

EXPENSE SHEETS

CASE NAME: _____
FILE NUMBER: _____

DATE PAID	CHECK #	PAYABLE TO	BILL DATE	AMOUNT	OTHER

PERSONAL INJURY CASE INFORMATION FORM

A.   CLIENT INFORMATION

NAME:	Social Security Number:
PHONE NO.:	Date of Birth:
ADDRESS:	D.O.I.
TOWN:	ACCIDENT DESCRIP:

INJURIES:

B.   INSURANCE INFORMATION

CLIENT INSURANCE:	OTHER:
ADDRESS:	ADDRESS:
ADJUSTER:	ADJUSTER:
MEDPAY:	DRIVER:
INSURED:	INSURED:
POLICY LIMITS:	POLICY LIMITS:

C.   MEDICAL PROVIDERS/HOSPITAL

PROVIDER:
ADDRESS:
PHONE NUMBER:
RATING, IF ANY:
TOTAL MEDICAL BILLS:
TOTAL UNPAID BILLS:

PROVIDER:
ADDRESS:
PHONE NUMBER:
RATING, IF ANY:
TOTAL MEDICAL BILLS:
TOTAL UNPAID BILLS:

PROVIDER:
ADDRESS:
PHONE NUMBER:
RATING, IF ANY:
TOTAL MEDICAL BILLS:
TOTAL UNPAID BILLS:

PROVIDER:
ADDRESS:
PHONE NUMBER:
RATING, IF ANY:
TOTAL MEDICAL BILLS:
TOTAL UNPAID BILLS:

PROVIDER:
ADDRESS:
PHONE NUMBER:
RATING, IF ANY:
TOTAL MEDICAL BILLS:
TOTAL UNPAID BILLS:

PROVIDER:
ADDRESS:
PHONE NUMBER:
RATING, IF ANY:
TOTAL MEDICAL BILLS:
TOTAL UNPAID BILLS:

D.   LOST WAGES

EMPLOYER NAME:
EMPLOYER ADDRESS:
OF LOST DAYS:
SALARY/WAGES:

E.   PROPERTY DAMAGE

TOWING:
ESTIMATE OF DAMAGES:
PAID/UNPAID:

DEPOSITION SUMMARY

DEPOSITION SUMMARY			Case:	Date of Depo	Deponent
PAGE#	LINE#	ISSUE			SUMMARY

HOLD HARMLESS AGREEMENT

PLAINTIFF:

DEFENDANT:

PREMISES:

DATE:

The undersigned hereby agree as follows:

1. The Plaintiff will enter the above property for the purpose of:

2. That in consideration of permission to grant entry onto said premises, Plaintiff and any further person accompanying the Plaintiff agrees to do the following:

    a. To hold harmless and indemnify the Defendant and/or any owner of the premises from any claims for personal injuries or property damage resulting from Plaintiff's entry onto the premises.

    b. To be solely responsible for the cost and any expenses associated with the purpose of entry.

    c. The Plaintiff acknowledges that s/he is aware that s/he does not have permission to access the property for any other purpose other than that states above.

_____   _____
PLAINTIFF   DEFENDANT

Date: _____   **Date:** _____

AFFIDAVIT OF NO HEALTH INSURANCE

1. I certify that at the time of this accident, there was no health insurance or Automobile/medical payment policy in effect that would provide coverage for medical bills I have incurred as a result of this loss.

Subscribed and sworn to before me this __ day of _____.

Witness _____   _____
                                      Uninsured party

Witness _____

State of _____

County of _____   __/___/200__

Personally Appeared _____
Signer of the foregoing Instrument, and acknowledged the same to be his or her free act and deed, before me.

_____
Commissioner of the Superior Court/Notary Public

2. I certify that at the time of this accident, there was no health insurance/medical payment policy in effect that would provide coverage for medical bills I have incurred as a result of this loss except for health insurance through Title XIX, which is repayable.

Subscribed and sworn to before me this __ day of _____.

Witness _____   _____
                                      Uninsured party

Witness _____

State of _____

County of _____   __/___/200__

Personally Appeared _____
Signer of the foregoing Instrument, and acknowledged the same to be his or her free act and deed, before me.

_____
Commissioner of the Superior Court/Notary Public

AFFIDAVIT OF NO AUTOMOBILE INSURANCE

I, _____ of _____ , being duly sworn, hereby depose and say:

1.   That I am over the age of eighteen years and believe in the obligation of an oath.

2.   That I am the owner of a (YEAR MAKE & MODEL) which was involved in a motor vehicle accident on or about _____.

3.   At the time of said motor vehicle accident, I did not maintain a policy of automobile insurance which would provide benefits to pay any medical bills, property damage claim, or personal injury claim incurred as a result of said accident.

_____

Subscribed and Sworn to before me this __ day of _____.

_____
Notary Public

My Commission Expires:

SETTLEMENT STATEMENT FOR PERSONAL INJURY CLAIM

RE: CASE NAME
        DATE OF LOSS:

FULL AND FINAL SETTLEMENT $
LESS:
ATTORNEY'S FEES   ($.)

LESS COSTS
Copies of medical records   ($.)
Postage   ($.)

OUTSTANDING MEDICAL EXPENSES:
Provider #1 $
(bill compromised $)
Provider #2 $
(bill compromised $)
Provider #3 $
(bill compromised $)
TOTAL MEDICALS $ ($.)

TOTAL DEDUCTIONS: ($.)

TOTAL DUE TO CLIENT: $

_____
CLIENT SIGNATURE   DATE

RELEASE OF ALL CLAIMS

TO ALL TO WHOM THESE PRESENTS SHALL COME OR MAY CONCERN,

 GREETING: KNOW YE, That _____ of _____ (hereinafter referred to as the Releasor) for and in consideration of the sum of _____ **AND 00/100 ($ _____) DOLLARS** and other valuable consideration paid to the Releasor by_____ (hereinafter referred to as the Releasee), the receipt of which is hereby acknowledged, has remised, released and forever discharged, and by these Presents does remise, release and forever discharge the Releasee of and from all actions, bonds, causes of action, claims, contracts, covenants, damages, debts, demands, disputes, endorsements, executions, judgments, obligations, promises, suits, or trespasses, in law or in equity, which against the Releasee, the Releasor ever had, now has or hereafter can, shall, or may have, for, upon or by reason of any matter, cause or thing whatsoever, from the beginning of time to the date hereof.

 Any and all claims for damages resulting from personal injuries sustained on _____ .

The undersigned agrees to hold _____ , their heirs, representatives, successors and assigns harmless from any liens including but not limited to liens asserted by any self-funded plan, ERISA plan, or any other insurance provider and/or payor of benefits.

 IN WITNESS WHEREOF, the Releasor has executed this instrument on _____ , **2009.**

_____   _____

_____

STATE OF _____

         Social Security Number: _____

COUNTY OF _____

 Personally appeared _____ signer and sealer of the foregoing instrument, and acknowledged the same to be his free act and deed before me.

        _____

        Commissioner of the Superior Court

EMPLOYEE APPLICATION

PERSONAL INFORMATION:

First Name: _____ Middle Name: _____

Last Name: _____

Street Address: _____

City, State, Zip Code: _____

Phone Number: Home: (___)_____ Cell: (___)_____

E-mail Address: _____

Are you eligible to work in the United States?

Yes _____ No_____

Have you been convicted of or pleaded no contest to a felony within the last five years?

Yes_____ No_____

If yes, please explain: _____

_____

POSITION/AVAILABILITY:

Position Applied For:_____

Days/Hours Available:

Monday _____
Tuesday _____
Wednesday _____
Thursday _____
Friday _____
Hours Available: from _____ to _____

What date are you available to start work?_____

EDUCATION:

Name and Address of School - Degree/Diploma - Graduation Date

_____

_____

_____

_____

_____

Skills and Qualifications: Licenses, Skills, Training, Awards

_____

_____

EMPLOYMENT HISTORY:

Present or Last Position:

Employer: _____

Address:_____

Supervisor: _____

Phone: _____

E-mail: _____

Position Title: _____

From: _____ To: _____

Responsibilities: _____

_____

Salary: _____

Reason for Leaving: _____

Previous Position:

Employer: _____

Address:_____

Supervisor: _____

Phone: _____

E-mail: _____

Position Title: _____

From: _____ To: _____

Responsibilities: _____

_____

Salary: _____

Reason for Leaving: _____

May We Contact Your Present Employer?

Yes _____ No _____

References:

Name/Title Address Phone

_____

_____

_____

I certify that information contained in this application is true and complete. I understand that false information may be grounds for not hiring me or for immediate termination of employment at any point in the future if I am hired. I authorize the verification of any or all information listed above.

Signature_____

Date_____

BIBLIOGRAPHY

1. TAKING THE PLUNGE

ARTICLES

Bathija, Sandhya. "When Handing a Shingle, Solos Are Reluctantly Solo." *The National Law Journal*, April 5, 2007.

Goldman, Andrea. "Offshoots of Practice." *GPSolo Magazine*, July/August 2005.

Hall, Douglas T. "Protean Careers of the 21st Century." *Academy of Management Executive*, November 1996.

Leffler, David. "Seven Secrets to Running a Better Solo Law Practice." *GPSolo Magazine*, April/May 2007.

Ravdin, Linda J. "Looking For Mr. (Or Ms.) Right: How to Choose A Law Partner." *GPSolo Magazine*, July/August 2004.

Sellers, Patricia. "The Liberating Effect of Failure." *Fortune Magazine*, May 29, 2008.

BOOKS

DuBrin, Andrew J. *Applying Psychology: Individual & Organization Effectiveness*, 5th ed. New Jersey: Prentice Hall, 2000.

George, Bill. *Authentic Leadership: Rediscovering the Secrets to Creating Lasting Value.* California: Jossey-Bass, 2003.

Holmes, Ann M. *There's a Business in Every Woman.* New York: Random House Publishing, 2007.

Ruderman, Marian N. *Standing at the Crossroads: Next Steps for High-Achieving Women.* Oregon: Beyond Words Publishing, Inc., 2002.

2. SETTING UP SHOP

ARTICLES

"How to Evaluate Your Office Leasing Needs." *Texas Bar Journal*, Vol. 71, No.7.

"How to Write and Implement a Law Office Business Plan." *Texas Bar Journal*, Vol. 71, No.7.

"Looking For Mr. (Or Ms.) Right: How to Choose a Law Partner." *GPSolo Magazine*, July/August 2004.

Rivera, Rudy. "Developing a Niche Practice." *GPSolo Magazine*, January/February 2007.

Schultz, Suzette and Jon. "Small Spaces: A Planning Primer for Solo and Small Firm Office Design." *GPSolo Magazine*, September 2005.

"Setting Up a Home Office." *GPSolo Magazine*, January/February 2007.

"Seven Secrets to Running a Better Solo Law Practice." *GPSolo Magazine*, April/May 2007.

Books

King, Ruth. *The Ugly Truth about Small Business*. Illinois: Sourcebooks, Inc., 2005.

Lasser, J.K. *How to Run a Small Business*. New York: McGraw-Hill, Inc. 1994.

Mancuso, Anthony. *LLC or Corporation? How to Choose the Right Form for Your Business*. California: Nolo, 2007.

Online

"Business Plan Outline."
http://sbinfocanada.about.com/cs/businessplans/a/bizplanoutline.htm.

3. Money Matters

Books

Lasser, J.K. *How to Run a Small Business*. New York: McGraw-Hill, Inc., 1994.

Online

"Building a Financial Budget." http://www.entrepreneur.com/article/printthis/21942.html.

"Cash (Flow) Really is King." http://www.enterpreneurs.about.com/od/beyondstartup/a/cashflow101.htm.

"Creating Your Business Plan Financials." http:www.sbinformation.about.com/od/ businessplans/a/bplanfinancials.htm.

"Estimating Realistic Start-Up Costs." http://articles.bplans.com/index.php/business-articles/starting-a-business/estimating-realistic-startup-costs.html.

"How Much Money Do You Need For a Start-Up?" http://www.wachovia.com/small_biz/pge/0,,447_972_1694_1831_1928,00.html.

Internal Revenue Service.
www.irs.gov.

"Start-Up Financing." http://www.entrepreneur.com/money/howtoguide/article52718.html.

"What is a Cash Flow Statement." http://www.investpedia.com/articles/04/033104.asp

4. From Pixels to Paper

ARTICLES

Bell, Terri. "The Virtual Office." *GPSolo Magazine*, June 2007.

Kodner, Ross L. "The $5,000 Law Office: Ferrari Performance on a Chevy Budget." *GPSolo Magazine*, April/May 2002.

Masur, Steven. "Confidentiality in a High-Tech World." *GPSolo Magazine*, July/August 2007.

Smith, Michael C. "Starting a New Law Office: A Checklist." *Texas Bar Journal*, Volume 71, Number 7.

BOOKS

Winston, Stephanie. *The Organized Executive*. New York: Warner Business Books, 2001.

ONLINE

"Data Backup is the Best Data Protection." http://sbinfocanada.about.com/cs /management/a/databackup.htm?p=1.

"Guide to Essential Computer Software for Business." http://work.com.

"Guide to Selecting the Right Start-up Technology." http://www.work.com.

"Guide to Selecting the Right Computer Hardware Configuration." http://www.work.com.

5. Dare to Be Different: Marketing Your Practice

ARTICLES

Calloway, Jim. "Marketing Magic for Lawyers." *GPSolo Magazine*, April/May 2002.

Zwicker, Milton W. and Anderson, Wells H. "Attract New Clients with Effective E-Newsletters." *GPSolo Magazine*, December 2007.

7. Controlling Client Conflict

ARTICLES

Calloway, Jim. "Keeping 'Em Happy: The Secrets of Client Satisfaction." *GPSolo Magazine*, January/February 2007.

McCulloch, Anne, Schehl, Joanne, and Esch, Roxanne. "How to Think Like Your Client." *GPSolo Magazine*, April/May 2006.

Poll, Edward. "Exceeding Expectations: Creating More Value for Your Clients." *GPSolo Magazine*, April/May 2002.

BOOKS

Bisno, H. *Managing Conflict*. Beverly Hills, CA: SAGE Publications, 1988.

DuBrin, Andrew J. *Applying Psychology: Individual & Organization Effectiveness, 5th ed*. New Jersey: Prentice Hall, 2000.

Hocker, J.L. & Wilmot, W.W. *Interpersonal Conflict*. Dubuque, IA: Wm. C. Brown, 1991.

Rahim, M.A. *Managing Conflict: An Interdisciplinary Approach*. New York: Praeger, 1989.

ONLINE

"Consumers Guide to Legal Malpractice." www.cobar.org.

OTHER

"Basic Considerations Regarding Lawyer Professional Liability Insurance." *Texas Bar Journal*, Vol. 71, No.7.

8. SETTING AND COLLECTING FEES

ARTICLES

Baker, Ronald J. "Your Firm Needs to Offer Fixed Prices." *The Complete Lawyer*, Volume 4, Number 5.

Ravdin, Linda J. "How to Weed Out Deadbeats." *GPSolo Magazine*, April/May 2002.

Trautz, Reid and McLaughlin, Paul. "Fee or Free: How Much Pro Bono Is Enough?" *GPSolo Magazine*, April/May, 2002.

BOOKS

Foonberg, Jay G., *How to Start & Build a Law Practice, 5th Edition*, Chicago, IL: American Bar Association Book Publishing, 2004.

9. WINNING THE WAR ON CHAOS: TIME AND PAPER MANAGEMENT

ARTICLES

Ball, Craig. "Practice Management: Technology and the Power of Persuasion." *GPSolo Magazine*, March 2004.

Foonberg, Jay G. "Preservation of Files Destroy or Not to Destroy." *GPSolo Magazine*, July/August 2007.

Kelly, Natalie R. "Case Management and Document Management Retooling Law Office Information." *GPSolo Magazine*, June 2007.

Masur, Steven. "Confidentiality in a High-Tech World." *GPSolo Magazine*, July/August 2007.

West, Robin Page. "Complex Litigation for Small Firms and Solo Lawyers." *GPSolo Magazine*, October/November 2003.

BOOKS

Bisno, H. *Managing Conflict*. Beverly Hills: SAGE Publications, 1988.

Covey, Stephen, Dr. *The Seven Habits of Highly Effective People*. New York: Simon & Schuster, 1989.

Hocker, J.L. & Wilmot, W.W. *Interpersonal Conflict*. Dubuque, IA: Brown, 1991.

Rahim, M.A. *Managing Conflict: An Interdisciplinary Approach*. New York: Praeger, 1989.

Winston, Stephanie. *The Organized Executive*. New York: Warner Business Books, 2001.

ONLINE

"3 Steps to Creating a Document Management System." http://sbinfocanade.about.com/od/datamanagement/a/documentmgt1.htm?p=1

OTHER

Morris, Jackie and Myers, Gayle. "Opening and Maintaining Client Files." *The Law Society of British Columbia*, June 2006.

10. TO STAFF OR NOT TO STAFF

ARTICLES

Calloway, Jim. "Care & Feeding of the Law Office Staff." *GPSolo Magazine*, January/February 2007.

"How to Draft an Employee Handbook." *Texas Bar Journal*, Vol. 71, No.7.

BOOKS

Lasser, J.K. *How to Run a Small Business.* New York: McGraw-Hill, Inc., 1994.

Winston, Stephanie. *The Organized Executive.* New York: Warner Business Books, 2001.

11. THE MISNOMER OF BALANCE

BOOKS

DuBrin, Andrew J. *Applying Psychology: Individual & Organization Effectiveness, 5th ed.* New Jersey: Prentice Hall, 2000.

Hirshon, Robert. Preface to *Balanced Lives: Changing the Culture of Legal Practice*, The ABA Commission on Women in the Profession, September 2001.

ONLINE

"Keeping Plates in the Air: How to Attain Work-Life Balance." http://www.emmerichfinancial.com.

"Lawyer Assistance Program Frequently Asked Questions." http://calbar.ca/gov.state/calbar/calbar_generic.jsp?cid=10566&id=25561.

OTHER

"Initial Report on the Survey: Work/Life Balance in the Legal Profession." Work Life Balance Task Force, Oklahoma County Bar Association. April 2003.

"Report of the AALS Special Committee on Problems of Substance Abuse in the Law School." Committee of the Association of American Law Schools. May, 1993.

"Seventh Special Report to U.S. Congress on Alcohol and Health from the Secretary of Health and Human Services." National Institute on Alcohol Abuse and Alcoholism. 1990.

13. LIPSTICK IN A BRIEFCASE: THE FEMALE SOLO PRACTITIONER

ARTICLES

Hockett, Rob. "14 Financial Facts and Consequences for Women." *The Complete Lawyer*, Volume 4, Number 2.

Ostrow, Ellen. "Women Lawyers & Business Development." *The Complete Lawyer*, Volume 1, Number 3.

BOOKS

Frankel, Lois P. *See Jane Lead*. New York: Warner Business Books, 2007.

Holmes, Ann M. *There's a Business in Every Woman*. New York: Random House Publishing, 2007.

Lichtenberg, Ronna. *Pitch Like a Girl*. New York: Rodale, 2005.

Ohlott, Patricia J. and Ruderman, Marian N. *Standing at the Crossroads: Next Steps for High-Achieving Women*. San Francisco: Jossey-Bass, 2002.

ONLINE

"Professional Women: Vital Statistics." http://www.dpeaflcio.org/programs/factsheets/fs_2008_Professional_Women.htm.

"Women Lawyers Salaries Slipping: Billing Rates Are Lower Than Male Lawyers." http://almresearchonline.typepad.com.

OTHER

"Sharing What We Know: A Resource for and by Heller Ehrman Women." Heller Ehrman, 2005.

ABOUT THE AUTHOR

RENÉE CAGGIANO BERMAN was born in Massachusetts on June 27, 1977. Prior to pursuing a legal education, Attorney Berman worked as a legislative advocate and media and political consultant for private and non-profit organizations. Attorney Berman attended Suffolk University Law School and the University of Connecticut. In September 2007, she opened a practice devoted to family law in Connecticut. She is currently a member of the Greater Bridgeport Bar Association, the New Haven County Bar Association, and the Connecticut Bar Association (Family Law Section). She is also a member of her local Chamber of Commerce. Since 2004, Attorney Berman has provided pro bono services to clients through the Connecticut Pro Bono Network. She is admitted to practice law in Connecticut and the United States District Court for the District of Connecticut. Her practice can be found on the Web at www.berman-lawct.com. She can be e-mailed at rberman@bermanlawct.com.